WORKBOOK

FUTURE 2

English for Work, Life, and Academic Success

Second Edition

Series Consultants
Sarah Lynn
Ronna Magy
Federico Salas-Isnardi

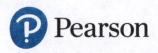

Future 2 Workbook
English for Work, Life, and Academic Success

Pearson Education, 221 River Street, Hoboken, NJ 07030 USA

Staff credits: The people who made up the *Future 2 Workbook* team, representing content development, design, manufacturing, marketing, multimedia, project management, publishing, rights management, and testing, are Pietro Alongi, Jennifer Castro, Dave Dickey, Gina DiLillo, Warren Fischbach, Pamela Fishman, Gosia Jaros-White, Joanna Konieczna, Michael Mone, Mary Perrotta Rich, Katarzyna Starzyńska-Kościuszko, Claire Van Poperin, Joseph Vella, Gabby Wu.

Text composition: Dataflow International
Cover design: EMC Design Ltd
Audio: CityVox

ISBN-13: 978-0-13-454760-2
ISBN-10: 0-13-454760-8

Printed in the United States of America

13 2022

CONTENTS

TO THE TEACHER

The *Future 2 Workbook* has 12-page units to complement what students have learned in the Student Book. Each Workbook unit follows the lesson order of the Student Book and provides supplemental practice in vocabulary, life skills, listening, grammar, reading, and writing. Students can complete the exercises outside the classroom as homework or during class time to extend instruction.

The Workbook audio provides practice with conversations, grammar, and workplace, life, and community skills competencies. In addition, the audio includes the readings from the Workbook so students can become more fluent readers.

UNIT STRUCTURE

Vocabulary
Practice focuses on the vocabulary presented on the first spread of the unit. Typical activities are word and sentence completion, labeling, and categorizing. Some lessons include sentence writing to reinforce the lesson's vocabulary, and some lessons include personalized exercises.

Grammar and Listening
Grammar is the main focus, with listening practiced as well. Grammar is practiced in contextualized exercises that include sentence completion, sentence writing, sentence scrambles, matching, and multiple choice. Listening activities include listening comprehension, listening dictation, and listening to check answers. Some lessons include vocabulary exercises to reinforce the new vocabulary taught in the lesson. Some lessons include personalized activities.

Workplace, Life, and Community Skills
In the second edition, the Life Skills lesson has been revised to focus on workplace, life, and community skills and to develop the real-life language and civic literacy skills required today. Lessons integrate and contextualize workplace content. In addition, every lesson includes practice with digital skills on a mobile device.

Writing
In the second edition, a cumulative writing lesson has been added to every unit. This new lesson requires students to synthesize and apply their learning in a written outcome. Through a highly scaffolded approach, students begin by analyzing writing models before planning and finally producing written work of their own.

Reading
All reading lessons have new, information-rich texts and a revised pedagogical approach in line with the CCR and ELP standards and the NRS descriptors. These informational texts are level appropriate, use high-frequency vocabulary, and focus on interpretation of graphic information. The readings build students' knowledge and develop their higher-order reading skills by teaching citation of evidence, summarizing, and interpretation of complex information from a variety of text formats.

Soft Skills at Work
Future has further enhanced its development of workplace skills by adding a Soft Skills at Work lesson to each unit. Soft skills are the critical interpersonal communication skills needed to succeed in any workplace. Students begin each lesson by discussing a common challenge in the workplace. Then, while applying the lesson-focused soft skill, they work to find socially appropriate solutions to the problem.

ADDITIONAL RESOURCES

At the back of the Workbook, you will find:
- Audio Script
- Answer Key

ORIENTATION

The Workbook, like the Student Book, includes an orientation for students. Before the students use the Workbook for the first time, direct them to To the Student on the next page. Go through the questions and tips with the students and answer any questions they may have so they can get the most out of using the Workbook.

TO THE STUDENT

LEARN ABOUT YOUR BOOK

A Look in the back of your book. Find each section. Write the page number.

Audio Script ___   Answer Key ___

B Look at page 152. Find *Answers will vary*. What does *Answers will vary* mean?

C Where is the audio?

D Look at page 5. What does ▶ mean?

TIPS FOR USING THE AUDIO

Read the tips for using the audio.

- For all exercises, listen to each track many times.
- For dictation exercises, use the pause button so you can have more time to write.
- After you finish the unit, play the audio again and read the audio script in the back of the book at the same time.
- Also, for more listening practice, listen to the conversations and readings when you are in the car or on the bus.

WRITING TIPS

Read the writing tips.

- Start sentences with a capital letter.
- End statements with a period (.).
- End questions with a question mark (?).

For example:

My name is Jack.

What's your name?

Unit 1: Making Connections

Lesson 1: Vocabulary

A Complete the chart. Use the words in the box.

~~a beard~~	~~average height~~	~~straight~~	~~short~~	~~average weight~~
curly	a goatee	heavy	long	a mustache
short	medium-length	tall	thin	wavy

Facial hair	Hair type	Hair length	Height	Weight
a beard	straight	short	average height	average weight

B Complete the sentences. Describe each person, using the words from Exercise A.

1. Sue has ___short___, ___straight___ hair.

2. Ahmed has _____, _____ hair.

3. Claire has _____, _____ hair.

4. Saul has _____, _____ hair.

1. Sue

2. Ahmed

3. Claire

4. Saul

C Look at the picture. Write words to describe the people.

Michael

short hair

_____

_____

_____

_____

Cha-Ram

_____

_____

_____

_____

Alex

_____

_____

_____

_____

D WRITE ABOUT IT. Write about four of your friends, family members, or classmates.

Alonso: short, average weight, curly hair

1. _____

2. _____

3. _____

4. _____

Lessons 2 & 3: Listening and Grammar

A Cross out the incorrect words.

1. **A:** Marta and Clara look alike!

   B: Yes, they both ~~has~~ / **have** blue eyes and red hair.

2. **A:** What does your brother look like?

   B: He **is / has** average height and a little heavy.

3. **A:** Are those girls your cousins?

   B: Yes, that's Gloria and Fatima.

   A: Wow! They **are / have** very attractive.

4. **A:** Is the man with the goatee your husband?

   B: No, he **isn't / aren't**. My husband **don't have / doesn't have** a goatee!

5. **A:** Look! That's Nina.

   B: No, Nina **doesn't have / don't have** blond hair.

   A: Well, she **is / has** blond hair today!

   B: Oh, yeah! That is Nina!

B Complete the sentences. Write the correct forms of *be* or *have*.

1. Mark **(not)** _doesn't have_ straight hair.

2. Nicole and Pilar _____ long, curly hair.

3. Mi-Hee _____ average height.

4. Mr. Johnson _____ a beard.

5. Carlos and Fernando **(not)** _____ heavy.

6. Mr. and Mrs. Johnson _____ good-looking.

7. I **(not)** _____ blond hair.

C ▶ Listen and circle *True* or *False*.

1. Carol has blond hair.   True   False
2. Carol has long, straight hair.   True   False
3. Carol has blue eyes.   True   False
4. Carol is average height.   True   False
5. Carol is heavy.   True   False
6. Carol is pretty.   True   False

D Look at the picture. Write sentences to describe the people.

Marco   Ernesto   Lisa   Kate   Viktor   Olga

1. *Marco has short hair.* _____

2. _____

3. _____

4. _____

5. _____

6. _____

Lesson 4: Workplace, Life, and Community Skills

A Look at the driver's license. What do the abbreviations mean?

1. APT _____apartment_____

2. DOB _____

3. F _____

4. HT _____

5. WT _____

6. BLK _____

7. BRN _____

Florida *The Sunshine State*

DRIVER LICENSE

S514-172-80-844-0

CRUZ, NINA S
150 CLEARWATER ROAD APT. 5
TALLAHASSEE, FLORIDA 32317

DOB: 08-16-78   SEX: F   HT: 5-6

WT: 135   HAIR: BLK   EYES: BRN

ISSUED: 02-13-17   EXPIRES: 02-13-26

Nina S Cruz

B Look at the driver's license in Exercise A again. Complete the sentences.

1. Nina's last name is _____Cruz_____.

2. Nina lives on _____ Road.

3. Nina lives in the state of _____.

4. Nina was born in the year _____.

5. Nina is _____ feet, and _____ inches tall.

C Complete the application form with your information.

DMV   **DRIVER LICENSE / ID CARD APPLICATION**

LAST NAME		FIRST NAME		MIDDLE INITIAL	SUFFIX (JR., SR.)
DATE OF BIRTH (mm-dd-yyyy)	HEIGHT	WEIGHT	SEX (CIRCLE)	HAIR COLOR	EYE COLOR
	FT. IN.	lbs.	M F		
RESIDENCE ADDRESS	STREET				APT. #
CITY, STATE, ZIP CODE		SIGNATURE OF APPLICANT X			

Lessons 5 & 6: Listening and Grammar

A Complete the sentences. Cross out the incorrect word.

1. Tina tells great jokes **and** / ~~but~~ she's very funny.

2. Mr. Lee isn't friendly **and** / **but** he's bossy.

3. Marco is cheerful **and** / **but** his brother is moody.

4. Andrew writes great social media posts **and** / **but** he's very interesting.

5. Sandra has black hair **and** / **but** her children have brown hair.

6. My manager is laid-back **and** / **but** he's friendly.

7. David and his father are heavy **and** / **but** his mother is slim.

8. Melissa doesn't have blue eyes **and** / **but** her sisters have blue eyes.

B Read what the people say about their personalities. Write two sentences about each person. Use *and* and *but*.

"I'm friendly. I'm a little shy. I think I'm funny. My friends say my blog is interesting."

Oscar

"I'm outgoing. I'm a little bossy. I'm talkative. I really like to tell stories."

Chung-Ho

1. _Oscar is friendly but he's a little shy._

   Oscar is funny and his blog is interesting.

2. _____

   _____

"I'm shy. I get nervous when I meet people. I love to travel. I love to visit new places and share photos."

Jason

"I am hard-working. I like to relax after work. I'm laid-back. My husband says I'm moody!"

Meg

3. _____

   _____

4. _____

   _____

A ▶ **Listen and read.**

HAS SOMEONE STOLEN YOUR IDENTITY?

Your identity has many parts. These include your name, your age, and your address. You also have a
5 social security number. The government uses this number to know who you are.

Your identity is valuable. People may try to steal it. This is
10 called identity theft. They can then buy things on your credit card.

How do you know if your identity has been stolen? Contact your bank if you:

• see unusual items on your bank statement or credit card bill.
15 • receive a bill for something you didn't buy.
• are unable to use your credit card.

So, how can you reduce the risk of identity theft?

Here are some tips:

How an identity is stolen in the U.S. (2017)

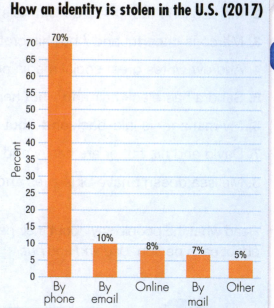

Category	Percent
By phone	70%
By email	10%
Online	8%
By mail	7%
Other	5%

Do	*Don't*
• Be careful with personal documents. Keep bank statements, bills, and medical records safe. • Be careful when sharing personal data (date of birth, email address, etc.) online. Not all websites are safe. • Check your bank statements regularly. It's important to discover any unusual charges as quickly as possible. • Shred credit-card offers that come in the mail.	• Use your social security number as identification. • Keep your social security card in your purse or wallet. • Put personal documents in the trash. Cut them up when you no longer need them. • Give out your personal information on the phone.

These simple steps can keep your personal information safe.

B **DEVELOP YOUR ACADEMIC SKILLS. Read the Academic Skill. Complete the sentences.**

1. The topic of the article is _____.
   a. paying with credit cards
   b. the best way to shop online
   c. protecting your identity

2. The main idea of the article is _____.
   a. it's impossible to be safe online
   b. you can take steps to protect your identity
   c. you should never shop online

> **Academic Skill: Identify the topic and the main idea**
>
> After you read, ask yourself, "What's the article about?" The answer is the topic of the article. Then ask, "What does the writer say about the topic?" The answer is the main idea.

C IDENTIFY. What is the main idea of the second paragraph?

    a. It's easy to steal an identity.

    b. You can protect your identity.

    c. Your identity is important.

D CITE EVIDENCE. Complete the sentences. Where is the information? Write the line number.

                                                                                               Lines

    1. Your identity includes information about your _____.

        a. job

        b. education

        c. location   _____

    2. If your identity is stolen, you might _____.

        a. get fewer statements

        b. see unusual charges

        c. not be able to use the internet   _____

    3. If you have old documents that show personal information, you should _____.

        a. give them to friends to keep safe

        b. take a photo of them

        c. cut them up   _____

E INTERPRET. Complete the sentences about the chart.

    1. In 2017, most people had their identity stolen _____.

        a. over the phone

        b. by email

        c. on a website

    2. _____ of all cases of identity theft involved e-mail and the internet.

        a. 5%

        b. 18%

        c. 70%

    3. The "Other" section is for identity theft that _____.

        a. happened in other ways

        b. happened in other years

        c. happened more than once

Lessons 8 & 9: Listening and Grammar

A Write questions. Put the words in the correct order.

1. (Pam / friendly / is)   *Is Pam friendly?* _____

2. (from Mexico / are / Mr. and Mrs. Garcia) _____

3. (you / are / married) _____

4. (your school / where / is) _____

5. (how old / the students / are) _____

6. (is / who / your teacher) _____

7. (is / your birthday / when) _____

8. (your name / what / is) _____

B Complete the conversations. Use *am*, *is*, *are*, *am not*, *isn't*, or *aren't*.

1. **A:** Are we late for class?

   B: No, we ___*aren't*___. We're on time.

2. **A:** Is the English class in room 12?

   B: Yes, it _____. It's on the first floor.

3. **A:** Are you in this class?

   B: No, I _____. I'm in the morning class.

4. **A:** Are your children outgoing?

   B: No, they _____. They're shy.

5. **A:** Is Van from China?

   B: No, he _____. He's from Vietnam.

6. **A:** Are you the teacher?

   B: Yes, I _____. My name is Mr. Gordon.

7. **A:** Are Mr. and Mrs. Park talkative?

   B: Yes, they _____. They're very outgoing.

C Read the answers. Complete the questions.

1. **A:** Where _____is Ernesto from_____?
   B: Ernesto is from Chicago.

2. **A:** What _____?
   B: My phone number is 845-555-4398.

3. **A:** When _____?
   B: English class is at 2:00.

4. **A:** How old _____?
   B: My daughter is eight years old.

5. **A:** Who _____?
   B: My manager is Mr. Lee.

6. **A:** Where _____?
   B: I'm from El Salvador.

D Imagine you are meeting a new classmate. What questions could you ask? Write three *Yes / No* questions and three information questions. Use *be*.

Where are you from?

1. _____
2. _____
3. _____
4. _____
5. _____
6. _____

E WRITE ABOUT IT. Look at the questions you wrote in Exercise D. Answer the questions about yourself.

1. _____ 2. _____

3. _____ 4. _____

5. _____ 6. _____

Lesson 10: Writing

A Read the Writing Skill. Then circle the words that refer to steps in the sentences below.

1. (First,) I take the bus to town, and (then) I walk to the office.

2. First, open the box. Second, take out the food. Then, put it on the shelf.

3. I speak to the manager, and after that, I decide what to do.

4. To begin, you log in to your account. Then, you post the photo.

5. I walked to the store. Then, I went to the doctor. After that, I went to the drugstore.

> **Writing Skill: Introduce and explain steps of a routine**
>
> When you write about how to do something, explain each step. For each step, use words like *first*, *then*, and *after that*.
>
> (First,) I read a sentence aloud. (Then,) I record myself reading aloud. (After that,) I listen.

B Complete the paragraph.

~~first~~	then	after that	next

This is my routine when I apply for a job I'm interested in. ___First___, I read about the company online. _____, I find out what skills they are looking for. _____, I write a cover letter. _____, I send an email to the manager.

C Read the text. Correct three more errors.

am
I ~~is~~ a student. I need to get a new ID card. Second, I goes online to get the form. Then, I put the form in the mail. After then, I wait for my ID to arrive.

Lesson 11: Soft Skills at Work

A **BE INCLUSIVE.** How can you be inclusive at work? Check (✓) the correct answers.

❏ **a.** ask other people what they think

❏ **b.** don't listen to other people's opinions

❏ **c.** introduce yourself to new co-workers

❏ **d.** complain about co-workers

Meg works with many different people. She's friendly to everyone.

B Meg is planning a work party. Cross out the incorrect words.
Then circle *True* or *False*.

1. Meg: Our work party **is / are** on Saturday night. Are you coming, Ben?

Ben: **No / Yes**, I am. I can't wait!

Meg: Great! I have so much to do. **Then / First**, I have to check who can come. After that,

I need to find out if we have enough food.

Ben: Maybe I can help you.

Meg: Thank you! You are so **supportive / outgoing**!

2. Meg is inclusive.   **True**   **False**

C Meg meets one of her co-workers, Cheng. Cross out the incorrect words.
Then circle *True* or *False*.

1. Meg: Hi. Did you meet Martin, the new supervisor?

Cheng: Martin? **Is / Are** he short, with black hair?

Meg: No, he's tall and he **have / has** red hair.

Cheng: Oh, no, I didn't meet him, but I saw him this morning.

Meg: He's nice **and / but** very funny. I can introduce you to him, if you want.

Cheng: No, thanks. He seems outgoing but very **bossy / cheerful**.

2. Cheng is inclusive.   **True**   **False**

Unit 2: All in the Family

Lesson 1: Vocabulary

A Complete the chart.

aunt	brother-in-law	daughter-in-law	granddaughter
husband	mother	mother-in-law	wife
nephew	niece	sister	father-in-law

Related by birth	Related by marriage
aunt	brother-in-law

B Look at the Miller family tree. Write the family relationships.

1. Daniel and Sandra _husband and wife_

2. Karl and Gloria _____

3. Monica and Gloria _____

4. John and Sandra _____

5. Monica and Sally _____

6. Joseph and Tommy _____

7. Gloria and Sally _____

8. Daniel and Tommy _____

The Miller Family

Daniel — Sandra

Karl — Monica Gloria — John

Joseph Sally Tommy

C Look at the family tree in Exercise B. Complete the sentences.

1. Daniel and Sandra are Gloria's _____*parents*_____ .

2. Joseph and Sally are Monica's _____ .

3. Monica is John's _____ .

4. Karl is Tommy's _____ .

5. Daniel is Joseph's _____ .

6. Joseph is Sally's _____ .

7. Sally is Tommy's _____ .

8. Joseph is Gloria's _____ .

D **WRITE ABOUT IT.** Draw your own family tree. Start with one pair of your grandparents. Write each person's name and his or her relationship to you.

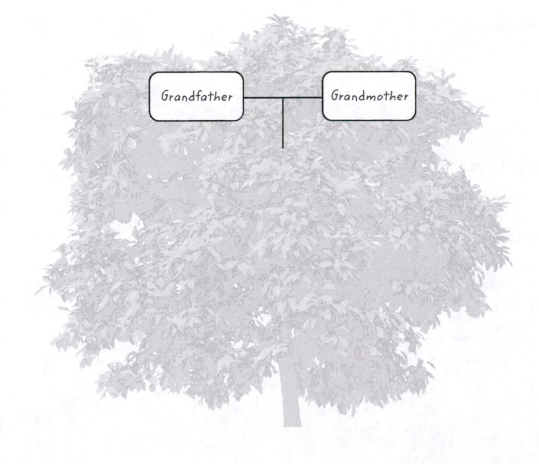

Lessons 2 & 3: Listening and Grammar

A Complete the sentences.

1. Sheila **(live)** _____lives_____ in California. She **(work)** _____ in a hospital.

   She **(have)** _____ a son.

2. Mr. and Mrs. Wang **(live)** _____ in New York City. They **(work)** _____ in a

   flower store. They **(have)** _____ two children.

3. Chin **(live)** _____ in Los Angeles. He **(work)** _____ at a bank.

   He **(have)** _____ a wife and a new baby.

4. My sister and I **(live)** _____ in a small town. We **(have)** _____ jobs after

   school. We **(work)** _____ in a restaurant.

B Write negative sentences. Use *don't* or *doesn't*.

1. Alice and Carlos live on Franklin Street.

   Alice and Carlos don't live on Franklin Street.

2. Sophia works in a hospital.

   _____

3. I have two jobs.

   _____

4. Deshi and Bo live in Florida.

   _____

5. You have four sisters.

   _____

6. Martin lives downtown.

   _____

C Complete the paragraph. Write the correct forms of the words.

My sister and I _____*live*_____ in Boston. I _____ in

  1. (live)   **2. (live)**

an apartment downtown. My sister _____ in a house

                                                          3. (live)

outside the city. I _____ in an office. My sister

                          4. (work)

_____ in an office. She _____ in a school.

5. (not work)   **6. (work)**

She and her husband _____ three sons but they

                                          7. (have)

_____ any daughters. My husband and I

8. (not have)

_____ any children yet. I'm happy that we

9. (not have)

_____ near my sister's family.

  10. (live)

D ▶ Listen. Read the sentences. Circle *True* or *False*.

1. Roberta has a new job.	True	False
2. Roberta works in a department store.	True	False
3. Roberta doesn't live near her job.	True	False
4. Roberta works in the evening.	True	False
5. Roberta has children.	True	False

E WRITE ABOUT IT. Think of two members of your family. Write sentences about each person's life and work.

My brother Sam lives in Los Angeles. He has two kids.

He works in a school.

1. _____

_____

2. _____

_____

A ▶ Listen and read.

FIND WORK/LIFE BALANCE WITH TECHNOLOGY

People today are busy at work and at home. Sometimes, we can forget to do important tasks because we are so busy. We also spend a lot less time with our friends or family. Luckily, technology can make us more organized. It can help us find a good work/life balance.

5 *Calendar* A phone calendar helps you become more organized. You can keep track of when you are working. You can also see holidays and family events like birthdays. Your phone can also send you reminders about these holidays and events so you can make plans for them.

Lists A list of things to do is useful. You can plan jobs at work. You can also plan
10 your days off. You can make a list of groceries or mail that needs to be sent. A list makes it easy to see what needs to be done. It helps you to organize and use your free time with friends or family well.

Apps There are lots of different apps that can help you get a better work/life balance. Some apps can help you get to work faster. They tell you if there are
15 traffic jams, or if there has been an accident. They can then tell you if there is a better route to take. There are also apps that show you how to get in shape if you don't have time to go to the gym. Other apps can help you relax if you are feeling stressed out.

B **DEVELOP YOUR ACADEMIC SKILLS.** Read the Academic Skill. Choose the best way to retell the information in these sentences.

Academic Skill: Retell information

Retell means to say in your own words what you read or hear. The words are different, but the meaning is the same.

1. "Technology can make us more organized."
   a. Using phones and computers can make us busier than ever.
   b. We can use technology to plan our time better.
   c. Technology can help us find a better job.

2. "A list of things to do is useful."
   a. Having a list makes you busy.
   b. Only list what is important.
   c. A list helps you get organized.

3. "Some apps can help you get to work quicker."
   a. Apps can help you find a shorter way to work.
   b. Never look at apps when you are driving.
   c. You can use apps at work.

C IDENTIFY. What is the main idea of the article?

    a. Technology can help you achieve work/life balance.

    b. Work/life balance is impossible to achieve.

    c. You need to work hard in order to succeed.

D CITE EVIDENCE. Complete the sentences. Where is the information? Write the line number.

Lines

1. Many people today _____ at work and at home.

    a. have a lot of responsibilities

    b. use too much technology

    c. think about their job   _____

2. A phone calendar can be useful because _____.

    a. it is easy to update with new events

    b. you can see all work and family events in one place

    c. it tells you how the traffic is   _____

3. Making a list makes it easier to _____.

    a. plan your time with your family

    b. relax when you're stressed out

    c. see when holidays are   _____

4. Some apps can help you _____.

    a. arrive at work on time

    b. tell co-workers you're going to be late

    c. get more holidays   _____

E WRITE ABOUT IT. Does technology help you organize your life better? Are there any ways that technology actually stops you from having a good work/life balance? Write three sentences about how technology affects your work/life balance.

_____

_____

_____

_____

_____

_____

A Match the answers to the questions.

1. Does Lan work in a Vietnamese restaurant? ___d___   a. Yes, they do.

2. Do your parents speak French? _____   b. No, we don't.

3. Does Frida live in Mexico? _____   c. Yes, I do.

4. Do we have a new car? _____   ~~d.~~ Yes, he does.

5. Do you work at night? _____   e. No, she doesn't.

B Cross out the incorrect words.

1. A: Do / ~~Does~~ Jason and you live in Miami?   B: Yes, we **do / does**.

2. A: Do / Does Yolanda work for a computer company?   B: No, she **don't / doesn't**.

3. A: Do / Does our parents live near a park?   B: Yes, they **do / don't**.

4. A: Do / Does Edward work from 8:00 to 5:00?   B: No, he **don't / doesn't**.

C Complete the conversations.

1. A: _____Does_____ your nephew _____live_____ in the United States?

   B: Yes, _____he does_____. My nephew lives here in Phoenix.

2. A: _____ you _____ a brother?

   B: No, _____. I have three sisters.

3. A: _____ Nelly _____ packages to her family in Puerto Rico?

   B: Yes, _____. She mails packages to her family every month.

4. A: _____ Hamza _____ with his cousins?

   B: Yes, _____. Hamza lives with his cousins in Chicago.

5. A: _____ Simon _____ any brothers?

   B: Yes, _____. He has two brothers.

6. A: _____ Alison _____ in a school?

   B: No, _____. She works in an office.

Lesson 7: Workplace, Life, and Community skills

A Look at the pictures. Write the words.

 1. l e t t e r

 2. l _ r _ e _ _ n _ _ o _ e

 3. _ _ c k _ g _

B Look at the charts. Then correct the information in the sentences.

Service	Package or letter	Speed	Service	Package or letter	Speed
Priority Mail Express	70 pounds or less	1 day	First-Class Mail	3.5 ounces or less for standard-sized envelopes 13 ounces or less for large envelopes and small packages	1-3 business days
Priority Mail	70 pounds or less	1-3 business days	Retail Ground	70 pounds or less	2-8 business days

Extra Mailing Services

Certificate of Mailing
You get a receipt to show you mailed the item on a certain date.

Delivery Confirmation
You can find out when your package is delivered.

Certified Mail
You get a receipt to show you mailed the item. You can find out when the item is delivered and who signed for it.

Insurance
If your package is lost or damaged, you get money back.

Registered Mail
You get a receipt to show you mailed the item. Your item is both certified and insured.

COD (Collect on Delivery)
The person who receives the item pays for the cost of mailing.

1. You can send a postcard by ~~Retail Ground~~. *First-Class Mail*

2. It takes 2-9 days for a Priority Mail Express letter to arrive. _____

3. You can send a 90-pound package by Priority Mail. _____

4. You can send a 12-ounce mailing tube by First-Class Mail. _____

5. With Certified Mail, the person you send the item to pays the cost of mailing. _____

6. With Delivery Confirmation, you get money back if the package is lost. _____

C ▶ Listen. Answer the questions.

1. What does the customer want to mail?
   a. a letter   **b.** a package   **c.** a large envelope

2. How does the customer send it?
   a. First Class   **b.** Retail Ground   **c.** Priority Mail

3. What extra mailing service does the customer want?
   a. Insurance   **b.** Certified Mail   **c.** Delivery Confirmation

D Read what each customer wants. What are the best services for each customer?

John needs to mail a large envelope. It needs to arrive in three days. The envelope weighs 10 ounces. He wants a receipt to show he mailed it. He also wants to know when it was delivered and who signed for it.

Mailing services: _____

Angela needs to mail a package. The package weighs 25 pounds. It needs to arrive in three days. She wants to get her money back if the package is lost.

Mailing services: _____

E WRITE ABOUT IT. Look up three different mailing service websites. Using the package details below, find out which company offers the lowest shipping rates to and from two U.S. addresses.

Package 1:

Weight: 5 pounds

3-4 business day delivery

Value: $20

Best rate and company:

_____

_____

Package 2:

Weight: 3 pounds

Next-day delivery

Value: $50

Best rate and company:

_____

_____

Package 3:

Weight: 1 pound

Same-day delivery

Value: $10

Best rate and company:

_____

_____

Lessons 8 & 9: Listening and Grammar

A Cross out the incorrect words. Then match the questions and answers.

1. Where ~~does~~ / do you live?   _e_   a. On the weekend.

2. How many sisters **do** / does she have?   ____   b. In the community center.

3. How often **do** /does you call your best friend?   ____   c. By text message.

4. Where does / **do** they study English?   ____   d. Every evening.

5. When do / **does** he visit his family?   ____   ~~e.~~ On Maple Street.

6. How do / **does** you keep in touch with your family? ____   f. Three.

B Write information questions about the underlined information.
Use *Which, When, Where, How, How many,* or *How often.*

1. **A:** _Where does Franco live?_ _____

   B: Franco lives <u>near the bus station</u>.

2. **A:** _____

   B: Dina works <u>at night</u>.

3. **A:** _____

   B: I have <u>ten</u> cousins.

4. **A:** _____

   B: Jackie emails her family <u>every day</u>.

5. **A:** _____

   B: My daughter lives in <u>San Diego</u>.

6. **A:** _____

   B: Mr. and Mrs. Shuh keep in touch with their son <u>by phone</u>.

7. **A:** _____

   B: Peter goes to class <u>three times a week</u>.

A Read the Writing Skill. Add capital letters and comma to names of places.

> **Writing Skill: Use capital letters and commas in names of places**
> Names of places begin with capital letters.
> For example: San Francisco
> Write a comma (,) between the name of a city and the name of a state or country. For example:
> Shenzhen, China
> San Francisco, California

1. I live in ~~las~~ ~~vegas,~~ ~~nevada.~~ *(L V N added above)*
2. The food came from new orleans louisiana.
3. The music was popular in chicago illinois.

B Look at the map. Complete the chart. Then write the name of the city and state.

Los Angeles · Chicago · Philadelphia · Dallas · Miami

City	State	City and state
Philadelphia	Pennsylvania	1. _Philadelphia, Pennsylvania_
_____	Illinois	2. _____
Miami	_____	3. _____
Dallas	_____	4. _____
_____	California	5. _____

C Read the text. Correct four more errors.

My Daughters

by Ana Ruiz

I have two ~~daughter.~~ *daughters* Maria lives in Mexico City Mexico, and Tina lives in detroit Michigan. I live in San Francisco, california but we keep in touch. We text each other every day. We also talk on the phone on weekends.

Lesson 11: Soft Skills at Work

A **SEPARATE HOME AND WORK LIFE. How can you separate work life from home life?**
Check (✓) the correct answers.

❑ **a.** check work email at home

❑ **b.** make personal phone calls at work

❑ **c.** relax in your free time

Bo is a server.
He has a new job
in a restaurant.

B Bo's supervisor wants Bo to work on the weekend. Cross out the incorrect words.
Then circle *True* or *False*.

1. Supervisor: Bo, **do / does** you have any plans this weekend?

Bo: Yes, I **do / does**. It's my daughter's birthday.

Supervisor: **When / Where** is it? Dita is sick. She can't work on Saturday.

Bo: It's on Saturday. My parents are coming for the party.

Supervisor: Okay, well, enjoy the visit. I'll ask someone else.

2. Bo separates his work and home life.   **True**   **False**

C Bo talks to Anna, a co-worker. Cross out the incorrect words. Then circle *True* or *False*.

1. Bo: **When / Where** does your daughter go to college?

Anna: In California. She **live / lives** in San Diego.

Bo: **Do / Does** you talk to her every day?

Anna: No, I **don't / doesn't**, but I text her often on my break.

Bo: It's great that you **has / have** a way to keep in touch.

Anna: True. It also helps me relax when I'm on my break!

2. Anna separates her work and home life.   **True**   **False**

D **JOB INFORMATION.** Bo is a server. Look at the information. Then choose *True* or *False*.

Education Required	No formal education required
Work Environment	Restaurants
Previous Experience	None required

1. Servers need to go to college.   **True**   **False**

2. You need experience to work as a server.   **True**   **False**

Unit 3: Lots to Do

Lesson 1: Vocabulary

A Write the names of the clothes.

boots	a coat	gloves	~~a jacket~~
a raincoat	a scarf	a sweatshirt	jeans

1. _a jacket_   2. _____   3. _____   4. _____

5. _____   6. _____   7. _____   8. _____

B Look at the pictures and write the clothing.

An umbrella

Servet   Yasmin

C WRITE ABOUT IT. What clothing are you wearing today?

_____

_____

Lessons 2 & 3: Listening and Grammar

A Cross out the incorrect words.

1. Let's go to the shoe store. I need ~~buy~~ / **to buy** some new shoes for work.

2. I can't buy a new coat today. I need **save** / **to save** some money first.

3. Mrs. Silva doesn't **spend** / **to spend** a lot of money on clothes. She shops at clearance sales.

4. Nancy wants **return** / **to return** her new skirt. She doesn't like it.

5. Oscar needs **leave** / **to leave** class at 3:00. He has a doctor's appointment.

6. Luz doesn't like her new red sweater. She wants **exchange** / **to exchange** it for another color.

B Complete the sentences.

1. Tara (**not / want / buy**) ____doesn't want to buy____ that raincoat. She doesn't like the color.

2. Olivia and Max (**not / need / return**) _____ these hats. Their children like them.

3. I (**not / need / drive**) _____ to the grocery store today. I can go tomorrow.

4. Julia and Sam only buy clothes that are on sale. They (**not / want / spend**) _____ a lot of money

5. She (**not / want / go**) _____ to the shoe store with you. She doesn't need any shoes.

C WRITE ABOUT IT. **What do you need or want to do today? Write three sentences.**

_____

_____

_____

Lesson 4: Workplace, Life, and Community Skills

A Look at the online order form. Circle *True* or *False*.

🛒 **Items in Your Cart**

		Quantity	Price
Item 1:	Men's gloves	1	$9.98
Item 2:	Men's scarf	1	$15.00

Subtotal: $24.98
Shipping: FREE
Tax: $1.49
Total $26.47

Payment Method 🟦 🔴 🟩 🟥
Secure credit card payment

*Credit card number   *Expiration date   *Security code
11122233355668899   05 / 22   111

1. The shopper orders three items.	True	False
2. The scarf costs $9.98.	True	False
3. Shipping costs $1.49.	True	False
4. The shopper pays with a credit card.	True	False
5. The site is a safe site to use your credit card.	True	False
6. The shopper's credit card expires in June.	True	False
7. The shopper has to pay sales tax.	True	False

B Look at the receipt. Answer the questions.

1. What is the name of the store on the receipt? _Clothes Mart_

2. How much (%) is the discount on the jacket? _____

3. How much is the jacket after the discount and before tax?

_____

4. What is the date on the receipt for the jacket? _____

5. How much is the jacket after tax? _____

6. How much money does the customer give the cashier for the

jacket? _____

```
CLOTHESMART

09/07/19
Women's Wear
1 corduroy jacket    $49.99
Discount 20%       -  9.99
Subtotal              40.00
Sales Tax 6%           2.40
Total                $42.40
CASH                  50.00
Change                $7.60
```

C Read the store ad. Circle the clothing items that are on sale.

Thursday, October 28th to Sunday, October 31st

◆CLOTHESMART◆

Big Fall Sale!

All men's and women's outerwear on sale!
Come see our low prices on clothes for children and teens!

Women's jacket 25% off!
Regular price: $25
Now: $18.75

Women's raincoat 30% off!
Regular price: $30
Now: $21

Men's jacket 35% off!
Regular price: $40
Now: $26

Children's sweatshirt
Everyday low price: $15.00

D Read the store ad in Exercise C again. Then check the receipts below. Circle the mistakes.

1.

Cole's Department Store

10/28/19

Women's Outerwear

1 jacket	$25.00
Discount 10%	− 2.50
Subtotal	22.50
Sales Tax 8%	1.80
Total	$24.30
Cash	25.00
Change	.70

2.

Cole's Department Store

10/31/19

Men's Outerwear

1 jacket	$40.00
Discount 35%	−14.00
Subtotal	26.00
Sales Tax 8%	2.08
Total	$28.08
Cash	30.00
Change	1.92

3.

Cole's Department Store

10/30/19

Women's Outerwear

1 raincoat	$30.00
Discount 20%	− 6.00
Subtotal	24.00
Sales Tax 8%	1.92
Total	$25.92
Cash	25.92
Change	.00

4.

Cole's Department Store

10/29/19

Children's Outerwear

1 sweatshirt	$25.00
Sales Tax 8%	2.00
Total	$27.00
Cash	30.00
Change	3.00

Lessons 5 & 6: Listening and Grammar

A Complete the email. Use the correct forms of *be going to* and the verbs.

> Hi Rosa,
>
> I'm happy you _'re going to visit_ us this weekend! Please come on Sunday because our
> **1. (visit)**
>
> family _____ busy on Saturday. We _____ some spring cleaning.
> **2. (be)** **3. (do)**
>
> Lucas _____ the laundry, and I _____ the bathroom. Our kids, Joseph
> **4. (do)** **5. (clean)**
>
> and Manny, _____ their rooms. In the afternoon, my mother-in-law
> **6. (clean)**
>
> _____ the kids to the movies. Lucas and I _____ the living room and
> **7. (take)** **8. (paint)**
>
> wash the floors. The house _____ beautiful when you see it on Sunday!
> **9. (look)**
>
> See you soon!
>
> Eva

B Read the email message in Exercise A again. Correct the mistakes.
Use the correct form of *be going to*.

1. Eva is going to relax on Saturday.

   _Eva isn't going to relax on Saturday. She's going to be busy._____.

2. Rosa is going to visit on Saturday.

   _____.

3. The children are going to clean the bathroom.

   _____.

4. Eva's mother-in-law is going to take Lucas to a movie.

   _____.

5. Lucas and Eva are going to paint the bedroom.

   _____.

6. Lucas and Eva are going to wash the floors on Sunday.

   _____.

C ▶ Listen. Write the missing words.

Irene: I can't wait for Jeff's birthday party tonight! Do I need to bring anything?

Cindy: Well, let's see. Scott _____ some ice cream on his way home from

work. Alex and Nina _____ pizza and soda. I _____

a cake.

Irene: Did you remember the decorations?

Cindy: Yes. My sister _____ balloons and party games.

Irene: Cake, ice cream, pizza, games . . . Sounds like it _____ a fun party!

Cindy: Oh no! I need to go to the store.

Irene: Why?

Cindy: I forgot something very important. I forgot to buy Jeff's birthday present!

D Read the class poll. Write sentences about the students' plans.
Use the correct forms of *be going to.*

Class Poll: What are you going to do after English class?

Student	Activity	Student	Activity
Pablo	hang out with friends	Ana	hang out with friends
Monica	clean her house	Max	get lunch at a deli
Ying	cook lunch for her kids	Bernard	go home and relax
James	go home and relax	Carlo	wash his car

1. Monica _____.

2. Pablo and Ana _____.

3. Ying _____.

4. James and Bernard _____.

5. Max _____.

6. Carlo _____.

 **A** ▶ **Listen and read.**

ONLINE SHOPPING

Shopping has changed in recent years. People still shop in local stores, but more and more people are shopping online. It has become very popular.

5 Online shopping is very convenient. In the past, people had to travel to a store. Now, they can order items online and have them delivered to their home.

Online shopping is good for people
10 who want to save money. People don't have to go from store to store to compare prices. They can easily check prices from different websites. There are also more choices. More and more
15 stores are now selling online.

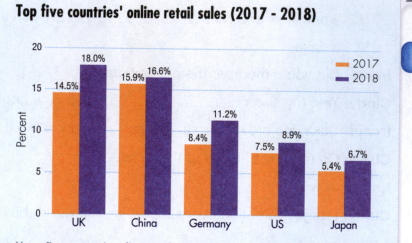

Top five countries' online retail sales (2017 - 2018)

Note: Percentage is online retail sales of total retail sales

In the past, it was difficult to know if a product or service was good. With social media, people can now read online reviews before they make a purchase.

Online shopping is convenient. However, there are some risks. Here are some basic guidelines when shopping online.

20 • Check that the website is safe before entering your credit card information.

• Look out for hidden charges – some stores have very high shipping fees.

• Find out the store's return policy.

B **DEVELOP YOUR ACADEMIC SKILLS. Read the Academic Skill. Complete the sentence.**

The author's purpose in this article is to _____.
    a. explain the dangers of online shopping
    b. show why online shopping is becoming more popular
    c. explain how a credit card can be used in different ways

Academic Skill: Identify purpose

Authors write articles for different reasons. This is the author's purpose. Knowing the author's purpose helps you understand the main idea.

C IDENTIFY. Which sentence from the text most closely relates to the main idea of the article? Circle the correct answer.

a. "Shopping has changed in recent years."
b. "Online shopping is very convenient."
c. "Find out the store's return policy."

D CITE EVIDENCE. Complete the sentences. Where is the information? Write the line number.

Lines

1. Online shopping is very useful if you are looking for items

that _____.
a. have the best prices
b. are hard to find
c. are unusual _____

2. When shopping online, you can use social media

to _____.
a. pay for your purchases
b. see what people say about the item
c. find the closest store _____

3. Before you enter your credit card information, you should _____.
a. try to find a cheaper item
b. write a review on social media
c. check that the website is safe _____

4. Although you can find great deals online, you need to watch out

for _____.
a. sales in your local store
b. extra charges for delivery
c. incorrect tax rates _____

E INTERPRET. Look at the bar graph. Complete the sentences.

1. In 2018, the percentage of online sales in the U.K. was about _____.
   a. 14.5%   b. 18.0%   c. 11.2%

2. In 2017, the percentage of online sales in Germany was _____ that of the U.S.
   a. higher than   b. lower than   c. the same as

3. In China, the percentage of online sales had increased by _____ from 2017 to 2018.
   a. 3.5%   b. 2.8%   c. 0.7%

4. In Japan, the percentage of online sales in 2017 was _____ that of 2018.
   a. higher than   b. lower than   c. the same as

Lessons 8 & 9: Listening and Grammar

A Cross out the incorrect words.

1. **A:** Are those shoes comfortable?

   B: No. I can't walk. They're **too** / ~~very~~ tight.

2. **A:** Where do you usually shop?

   B: There's a shopping mall near my house. It's **too** / **very** convenient.

3. **A:** Are you going with Terri to the clearance sale?

   B: No. She's going at 7:00 A.M. That's **too** / **very** early for me. I don't like to get up early!

4. **A:** Are you going to get the jacket?

   B: No. It's **too** / **very** pretty, but it's **too** / **very** expensive. I don't want to pay that much.

5. **A:** Should I buy this scarf?

   B: Yes, I think so. It's **too** / **very** cheap. It's not **too** / **very** late to get it.

B Complete the sentences. Write *too* or *very*.

1. These jeans don't fit. They are ____*too*____ big.

2. I like your new coat. It's _____ pretty.

3. I love wearing my new boots. They are _____ comfortable.

4. I don't want to wear my jacket today. It's _____ hot.

5. Merritt's department store is having a big clearance sale. The prices are _____ low.

6. The weather is _____ good today. It's not hot or cold.

C ▶ Listen. Identify why each person returns the clothing item. Circle the correct answer.

1. **a.** The pants are too short.   **b.** The pants are too big.

2. **a.** There's a hole in the jacket.   **b.** The jacket is too tight.

3. **a.** The shirt is too loose.   **b.** A seam is ripped.

4. **a.** A button is missing.   **b.** It's too big.

5. **a.** The boots are too big.   **b.** The boots are too tight.

D **What's wrong with each piece of clothing? Write sentences.**

1. _The hat is too small._

2. _____

3. _____

4. _____

5. _____

6. _____

7. _____

8. _____

Lesson 10: Writing

A Read the Writing Skill. Which paragraphs have a topic sentence? Circle the topic sentences.

1. (If you want to save money, go to many different stores.) Some stores are cheaper than others. Some have special offers and discounts too.

2. First, open a bank account. Second, save a certain amount every month. Third, try to save money for at least a year.

3. Beware of certain costs when shopping online. Shipping costs can be high. There might also be a processing fee.

> **Writing Skill : Use a topic sentence**
>
> Start your paragraph with a topic sentence. A topic sentence tells the main idea of the paragraph.
>
> For example:
>
> You can save money when you shop online.

B Read the paragraph. Circle the best topic sentence.

First, don't throw away your old clothes if they are ripped or have holes in them. Try to repair them rather than buying new ones. Consider buying used clothes from second-hand stores. Finally, remember that you don't have to buy new clothes every month!

a. It is easy to repair clothes.

b. Clothes are very expensive.

c. You can save money on clothing costs.

C Read the text. Correct three more errors.

In the past, I spent ~~very~~ *too* much money when I went shopping. Now I'm more careful. First, I don't buy something just because I like it. I might want buy it, but often I don't really need it. Second, I always check if there going to be a sale soon in the local stores before paying full price for something. Finally, I always check my change if I pay for something with cash. It's too easy for people to make a mistake.

Lesson 11: Soft Skills at Work

A LISTEN ACTIVELY. How can you listen actively? Check (✓) the correct answers.

❑ **a.** ask questions

❑ **b.** repeat to make sure you have understood

❑ **c.** don't interrupt

Rita is a salesperson at an electronics store.

B Rita is talking with a customer. Cross out the incorrect words. Then circle *True* or *False*.

1. Customer: I **want / want to** get a new tablet. My old one is **to / too** slow.

Rita: Okay. So you're **going / going to** buy a faster tablet. Is that right?

Customer: Yes. I hate it when videos take a long time to start playing.

Rita: Let's see if we can find the right tablet for you. This one is **very / too** fast.

2. Rita listens actively. **True** **False**

C Rita's co-worker asks her for help. Cross out the incorrect words. Then circle *True* or *False*.

1. Co-worker: I'm **too / very** late for a meeting. I **need / need to** go to the head office.

Do you know where it is?

Rita: I'm **going / going to** check for you. I'll be **too / very** quick.

Co-worker: Yes, please hurry.

Rita: You're going to the head office, right?

Co-worker: Yes.

Rita: Drive to Sullivan St. It's on the corner of Sullivan and Monk streets.

2. Rita is a good listener because she repeats to make sure

she understands. **True** **False**

D JOB INFORMATION. Read the information. Then choose *True* or *False*.

Job Title	Salesperson
Work Environment	Store
Facts	Many sales workers work evenings and weekends. About 1 in 3 retail salespeople worked part-time in 2016.

1. Most salespeople work full-time. **True** **False**

2. Salespeople only work during the day. **True** **False**

Unit 4: Small Talk

Lesson 1: Vocabulary

A Look at the pictures. Write the activities.

go dancing	~~go fishing~~	go for a bike ride	go for a walk
go running	go out to eat	go shopping	go swimming

1. _go fishing_

2. _____

3. _____

4. _____

5. _____

6. _____

7. _____

8. _____

B Complete the chart.

~~beach~~	bike ride	dancing	fishing
running	park	walk	zoo

go...	go to the...	go for a...
_____	_beach_	_____
_____	_____	_____
_____	_____	_____

C WRITE ABOUT IT. Answer the questions about your own activities.

1. What is your favorite outdoor activity? _____

2. What is your favorite indoor activity? _____

Lessons 2 & 3: Listening and Grammar

A Read the conversations. Cross out the incorrect words.

1. **A:** Is Martin doing well in his guitar class?

   B: No, he's not. He is **always** / ~~never~~ late for class, and he **never** / **always** practices.

2. **A:** My kids and I go for a bike ride every weekend.

   B: You're lucky. I hardly **ever** / **often** go for a bike ride. I'm too busy.

3. **A:** I'll make the kids a snack.

   B: Good idea. They're **usually** / **never** hungry after school.

4. **A:** What do you do in your free time?

   B: Well, I **sometimes** / **never** go to the movies with my friends. There's a great theater downtown.

5. **A:** My kids love to go to the zoo.

   B: My kids do, too. We **sometimes** / **hardly ever** spend the whole day there.

B Write sentences. Put the words in the correct order.

1. we / go fishing / usually / on Sundays

   We usually go fishing on Sundays.

2. always / goes dancing / on Saturday nights / Benita

   _____

3. for work / never / on time / Tom / is

   _____

4. in the summer / Ben and Janice / go hiking / often

   _____

5. my father / goes shopping / hardly ever

   _____

C Write questions with *How often*.

1. (the children / go swimming)   *How often do the children go swimming?*

2. (the family / go for a bike ride)   _____

3. (Dina / work late)   _____

4. (Alfredo and Dina / go out to eat)   _____

5. (the family / visit Grandma)   _____

D Look at the Lozado family's calendar. Answer the questions in Exercise C with complete sentences.

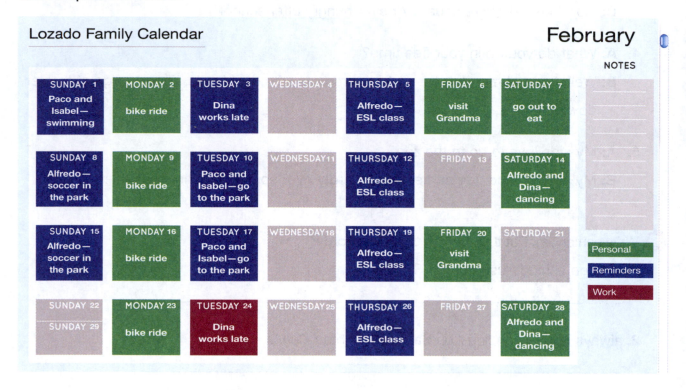

1. *The children go swimming once a month.* _____

2. _____

3. _____

4. _____

5. _____

Lesson 4: Workplace, Life, and Community Skills

A Look at the calendar. Complete the sentences about the events.

Rosemont Community Center   January

SUNDAY	MONDAY	TUESDAY	WEDNESDAY	THURSDAY	FRIDAY	SATURDAY
28	29	30	31	**Jan 1** computer class 1:00–3:00 P.M.	2 ESL class 9:00 A.M.–12:00 P.M.	Resume 3 Writing Workshop 11:00 A.M.–1:00 P.M.
4 Job Interview Workshop 8:00–10:00 P.M.	Job 5 Application Workshop 8:00–11:00 A.M.	citizenship 6 preparation class 6:30–8:30 P.M.	7 ESL class 9:00 A.M.–12:00 P.M.	8 computer class 1:00–3:00 P.M.	9 ESL class 9:00 A.M.–12:00 P.M.	Resume 10 Writing Workshop 11:00 A.M.–1:00 P.M.
11 Movie Club 8:00–10:00 P.M.	12	citizenship 13 preparation class 6:30–8:30 P.M.	14 ESL class 9:00 A.M.–12:00 P.M.	15 computer class 1:00–3:00 P.M.	16 ESL class 9:00 A.M.–12:00 P.M.	Resume 17 Writing Workshop 11:00 A.M.–1:00 P.M.
18 Job Interview Workshop 8:00–10:00 P.M.	19	citizenship 20 preparation class 6:30–8:30 P.M.	21 ESL class 9:00 A.M.–12:00 P.M.	22 computer class 1:00–3:00 P.M.	23 ESL class 9:00 A.M.–12:00 P.M.	Resume 24 Writing Workshop 11:00 A.M.–1:00 P.M.
25 Movie Club 8:00–10:00 P.M.	26	citizenship 27 preparation class 6:30–8:30 P.M.	28 ESL class 9:00 A.M.–12:00 P.M.	29 computer class 1:00–3:00 P.M.	30 ESL class 9:00 A.M.–12:00 P.M.	Resume 31 Writing Workshop 11:00 A.M.–1:00 P.M.

1. The ESL class meets on ___Wednesdays and Fridays___ from ___9:00___ A.M. to ___12:00___ P.M.

2. The citizenship preparation class meets every _____ at _____ P.M.

3. The Job Interview Workshop meets on the first and third _____ of the month from _____ to _____ P.M.

4. The Resume Writing Workshop starts at _____ A.M. and ends at _____ P.M.

B Look at the calendar in Exercise A again. Answer the questions.

1. When does the Job Application Workshop meet? _____

2. When does the Movie Club meet? _____

3. What time does the computer class start? _____

C ▶ Listen. When is each event? Circle the correct answer.

1. When is the dance class?
   a. The first Monday of the month from 7:00 to 9:00 P.M.
   b. The first and third Monday of the month from 7:00 to 9:00 P.M.

2. When is the English class?
   a. On Tuesdays and Thursdays from 5:30 to 7:00 P.M.
   b. On Tuesdays and Thursdays from 7:00 to 8:00 P.M.

3. When is the swimming class?
   a. On Wednesdays from 4:00 to 6:00 P.M.
   b. On Mondays and Wednesdays from 4:00 to 6:00 P.M.

4. When does the Walking Club meet?
   a. On Sundays from 7:00 to 8:00 A.M.
   b. On Sundays from 7:00 to 8:00 P.M.

5. When is the Movie Night?
   a. On Saturdays at 7:30 P.M.
   b. On Sundays at 7:30 P.M.

D Karima is a 22-year old sales assistant. She works from 9 A.M. to 5 P.M. and wants to improve her English. She checks her local library's website to see what classes it offers. Look at the website and check (✓) the filters that apply.

Lessons 5 & 6: Listening and Grammar

A Complete the sentences.

1. I **(like / take)** _____*like to take*_____ my lunch break at 1:30.

2. Ester **(not like / clean)** _____ her desk.

3. My husband **(hate / iron)** _____ the clothes.

4. Alex and Omar **(like / go)** _____ to meetings.

5. Sonya **(not like / stay home)** _____ on the weekends.

6. Mr. Patel **(like / work)** _____ outside when it's sunny.

7. Ivan **(hate / get up)** _____ early on Mondays.

8. Lara **(not like / swim)** _____ at the beach.

B Look at the information in the chart. Then complete each sentence.

	exercise	study	cook	get up early
Jackie	like	love	not like	not like
Jun	love	like	hate	like
Carmen	hate	not like	love	like
Paul	not like	love	not like	love

1. Jackie _____*likes to*_____ exercise.

2. Jun and Carmen _____ get up early.

3. Jackie and Paul _____ study.

4. Jackie and Paul _____ cook.

5. Carmen _____ study.

6. Paul _____ exercise.

7. Jun _____ cook.

8. Paul _____ get up early.

C ▶ Listen. Check (✓) the people who like each activity.

1.

	Rick	Angie
go hiking		
go to the beach		

2.

	Fred	Liz
eat Italian food		
go dancing		

D Look at Matt's web page. What does Matt like and dislike?
Write six sentences with *love* and *hate* and infinitives.

HOME   **MY PROFILE**   MY PHOTOS   MY FRIENDS

Personal Blog

Name: Matt

Location: Fort Worth, Texas

Things I love: fishing
swimming
doing karate
playing video games
walking my dog

Things I hate: getting up early
citizenship preparation
shopping

⬇ Download CV

★
VIEW BLOG

ABOT ME   VIEW RESUME   MY WORKS   CONTACT ME

1. _____.

2. _____.

3. _____.

4. _____.

5. _____.

6. _____.

A  **DEVELOP YOUR ACADEMIC SKILLS.** Read the Academic Skill. Look at the title and picture in the article. Complete the sentence.

This article is probably about _____.
    a. how people use social media at work
    b. how to fix a computer
    c. the dangers of communicating online

> **Academic Skill: Predict the topic**
> You can often guess what an article is about by looking at the title and any pictures. This will get you ready to understand what you read.

B ▶ Listen and read.

SOCIAL MEDIA IN THE WORKPLACE

Communication in the workplace has changed a lot. Ten years ago, people used email, phones, and texts to communicate. These technologies still exist. However, more and more workers are using social media. They
5 don't just use it to communicate with friends and family. It is important for business messages, too.

Why are things changing? First, many people think email is too formal. They also think it takes too long to write. By contrast, social media messages are usually very
10 short. They are perfect for quick messages. Most companies still use email, though. It is useful for explaining important messages in detail.

Second, in the past, photos from events were posted on company websites. People could not easily share them.
15 Today, colleagues use social media to share and "like" photos. They can write a short comment. They can also use emojis to show their reactions.

Finally, social media helps companies create online communities. They can show pictures and talk about new products with customers. Customers can also tell their stories. They can share their experience with a business
20 with others online.

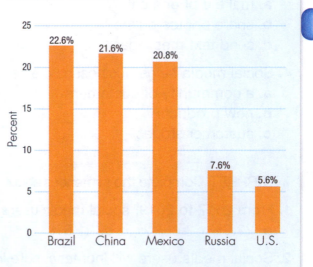

Estimated growth of social media users from 2017 to 2019

(Bar chart — Percent on vertical axis: Brazil 22.6%, China 21.6%, Mexico 20.8%, Russia 7.6%, U.S. 5.6%)

C **IDENTIFY.** What is the main idea of the article? Circle the correct answer.

a. How people use social media at work.
b. Social media is better than email.
c. Social media is good for formal communication.

D CITE EVIDENCE. Complete the sentences. Where is the information? Write the line number.

Lines

1. Ten years ago, employees mainly used _____ to communicate with each other.
   a. social media
   b. letters
   c. email   _____

2. Email is better than social media for _____.
   a. sharing photos
   b. liking a colleague's post
   c. providing lots of details   _____

3. In the past, it was more difficult to _____.
   a. make a phone call
   b. share photos online
   c. send text messages   _____

4. Social media helps businesses create _____.
   a. a community of customers
   b. new products
   c. customer stories   _____

E INTERPRET. Complete the sentences about the graph.

1. From 2017 to 2019, social media users in China will increase by _____.
   a. 22.6%   b. 21.6%   c. 20.8%

2. Social media users will increase more in _____ than in China.
   a. Brazil   b. Mexico   c. Russia

3. The growth of social media users in Russia will be _____ lower than that in Mexico.
   a. 13.2%   b. 7.6%   c. 1.6%

4. If we combine the growth of social media users in Russia and in the U.S., it is _____ the growth in China.
   a. higher than   b. lower than   c. the same as

Lessons 8 & 9: Listening and Grammar

A Complete the sentences. Use the infinitive forms of the verbs in the box.

~~cook~~	exercise	get up	meet	pay	take

1. We have plans to eat out tonight. I don't have ____*to cook*____ dinner.

2. Petar has _____ his new boss at 9:00 in the morning.

3. Lan wants to be healthy. She has _____ every day.

4. Roger drives his children to school. They don't have _____ the bus.

5. Parking is free on holidays. Drivers don't have _____ for parking.

6. Marie has _____ early during the week. She starts work at 6:30 A.M.

B Complete the conversation. Use the correct forms of *have to* and the words.

Chuck: Guess what? I got free tickets to the zoo. Do you and the kids want to go this Saturday?

Melinda: That sounds fun, but I __*have to work*__ this Saturday.
　　　　　　　　　　　　　　　1. (work)

Chuck: Oh. Do you have any plans on Sunday?

Melinda: Well, I don't, but Barry _____ to his guitar class. And Tina _____
　　　　　　　　　　　　　　2. (go)　　　　　　　　　　　　　　　　　**3. (play)**

in a soccer game. How about next Saturday? I _____ that day.
　　　　　　　　　　　　　　　　　　　　　　4. (not work)

Chuck: Hmm. Actually, I _____ my mother to a wedding. Can you go on Sunday?
　　　　　　　　　　5. (take)

Melinda: No, Sunday's not good. I _____ my sister. She's moving
　　　　　　　　　　　　　　　　　　6. (help)
to a new apartment.

Chuck: Oh, well. Too bad.

Lesson 10: Writing

A Read the Writing Skill. Then circle the details.

1. I enjoy healthy activities. I (walk) to work every day and I (use the stairs) instead of (the elevator).

2. My job is stressful. I often have to work extra hours.

3. I am trying to get in shape. I go to the gym three times a week.

4. I like hiking. My friends and I go hiking in the woods on weekends.

> **Writing Skill: Use details in your writing**
>
> Put details in your writing. Write details about time, people, and places. For example:
>
> No details: I love taking photos.
>
> With details: I love taking photos of (the mountains). I usually go on (Saturdays.) Sometimes, (my brother) comes with me.

B Read the text. Add details.

| ~~Sunday~~ | mountains | bike ride | evening | always |

I love to go hiking. Every _____Sunday_____ , my friends and I drive to the _____ nearby. We _____ bring sandwiches with us. Sometimes we go for a _____. We usually get home late in the _____.

C Read the text. Correct four more errors.

In my free time, I like ^to^ go dancing. I am usually go on Friday evening with my sister. My brother hardly goes. We go the school and dance with our friends. The dance alway finishes at 10:00 P.M.

Lesson 11: Soft Skills at Work

(A) **BE PROFESSIONAL.** How can you be professional? Check (✓) the correct answers.

❑ **a.** be polite

❑ **b.** complain

❑ **c.** arrive on time

Asad works in a supermarket.

(B) A customer asks Asad for help. Cross out the incorrect words. Then circle *True* or *False*.

1. Customer: I **am often / often** shop here. Can I ask you about something?

Asad: I'm going on my lunch break.

Customer: It's just a quick question. I **love / love to** cook pasta, but I can't find any fresh pasta here. Do you know if you sell it?

Asad: I **have / have to** go. Ask one of my co-workers.

2. Asad is professional. **True** **False**

(C) Asad talks with Justin, a co-worker. Cross out the incorrect words. Then circle *True* or *False*.

1. Asad: Justin, are you busy?

Justin: Yes, I **have / have to** clean the floor. I **am usually / usually** clean it before I leave.

Asad: I **hate / hate to** ask you, but there's a problem with my time sheet. Can you help me with it? I **hardly ever / am hardly ever** late with it.

Justin: Okay. I can do it now. And then I **have / have to** get back to cleaning the floor.

2. Justin is professional. **True** **False**

(D) **JOB INFORMATION.** Read the information. Then choose *True* or *False*.

Stock Clerks					
Percentile	10th	25th	50th	75th	90th
Hourly Wage	$9.07	$10.17	$11.77	$15.11	$19.40
Annual Wage	$18,870	$21,140	$24,470	$31,430	$40,360

1. Most stock clerks make about $24,000 a year. **True** **False**

2. The highest hourly wage is $19.04. **True** **False**

Unit 5: At Home

Lesson 1: Vocabulary

A Complete the conversations.

| leaking | no heat | ~~stuck~~ | working | no hot water |

1. **A:** It's hot in here. Could you open the window?

   B: I can't. It's _____ stuck _____.

2. **A:** It's very cold in the house.

   B: I know. There's _____.

3. **A:** There's water on the bedroom floor.

   B: I saw that. The ceiling is _____.

4. **A:** You can't wash the dishes.

   B: Why not?

   A: There's _____.

5. **A:** I'm going to the laundromat.

   B: Why? Is there something wrong with the washing machine?

   A: Yes. It's not _____.

B Look at the pictures. What are the problems?

1. ___ The door is stuck. ___

2. _____

3. _____

4. _____

5. _____

6. _____

Lessons 2 & 3: Listening and Grammar

A Cross out the incorrect words.

1. The plumber **is** / ~~are~~ fixing the sink.

2. I **are** / **am** calling an electrician to fix the lights.

3. Mr. and Mrs. Duran **is** / **are** going shopping for a new washing machine.

4. The building manager **is** / **are** buying a new radiator for our apartment.

5. Two faucets in the house **is** / **are** leaking.

6. You **am** / **are** using all the hot water. Don't take long showers!

7. You can cook now. The stove **is** / **are** working.

B Complete the sentences. Use the present continuous forms of the verbs.

1. Aldo _____*is painting*_____ the kitchen.
           (paint)

2. I think we need a new toilet. Hannah _____ to the plumber now.
                                          (talk)

3. Mark _____ an electrician. He _____ the building manager.
        (not call)   **(call)**

4. I _____ the building manager about the broken lock.
      (email)

5. Mary _____ at the ceiling, but she doesn't see the leak.
        (look)

6. The building manager _____ the clogged sink.
                         (not fix)

7. Cha-Ram is at the hardware store. She _____ a new lock.
                                          (buy)

8. I need to dry the laundry on the balcony. The dryer _____.
                                                       (not work)

9. I can't do the laundry. Someone _____ the washing machine.
                                    (use)

A Read the ad. Write the full word(s).

1. _____furnished_____   2. _____

3. _____   4. _____

5. _____   6. _____

7. _____   8. _____

9. _____   10. _____

11. _____   12. _____

13. _____   14. _____

15. _____   16. _____

17. _____   18. _____

Furn. 2 BR, 2 BA apt. on the second
   1   2   3   4
fl. No elevator. Large LR and DR.
5   6   7
Small EIK. Ht. and hw. not incl.
      8   9   10   11
W/D in bsmt. A/C. Nr. shopping and
12   13   14   15
trans. Parking on street. $1,400/mo.
16   17
   $700 sec. dep. Available May 1.
           18

Call Richmond Realty
222-555-9876.

B Read the ad in Exercise A. Correct the sentences.

1. The apartment has ~~three~~ _two_ bedrooms.

2. There is no furniture in the apartment.

3. The apartment has a large eat-in kitchen.

4. Hot water is included in the rent.

5. There is no air-conditioning.

6. The apartment is near a park.

7. The security deposit is one month's rent.

8. The rent is $1,500 a month.

9. There is parking behind the building.

C Read the utility bill. Answer the questions.

Portland Water

Dates of service:
June 2, 2019 – July 1, 2019

Name: Lin Guo   Meter number: 476392880

Date read:	07/02/2019
Number of days:	30
Usage:	35.6 units
Charges:	$114.68
Previous balance:	$72.55
Total:	$187.23

Due: 07/15/2019

1. What is the bill for? _____

2. Who is the bill for? _____

3. In what month was the meter read? _____

4. How many days does the bill cover? _____

5. How much water was used? _____

6. When should the bill be paid? _____

7. How much money needs to be paid? _____

D WRITE ABOUT IT. Marta, a co-worker, wants to move to your neighborhood. She lives with her husband and son. They don't have a car and they like to eat out. Find two apartments online for Marta and write sentences telling her about them.

_____

_____

_____

_____

Lessons 5 & 6: Listening and Grammar

A ► Listen. Complete the conversation. Write the words you hear.

Jackie: Hello?

Charlie: Hi, Jackie. This is Charlie at Richmond Realty. I have a nice _____ to show you.

Jackie: Great! Tell me about it.

Charlie: Well, it's really nice. There are three _____. And there's a large _____.

Jackie: How many _____ are there?

Charlie: Two.

Jackie: Is there a dining room?

Charlie: There's no dining room, but there's a big _____.

Jackie: Sounds good. How's the location? Is there a _____ nearby?

Charlie: Yes, there is. Right around the corner.

Jackie: And is the neighborhood quiet?

Charlie: Yes, it's on a very quiet street. There isn't a lot of _____.

Jackie: Wow. That sounds perfect. Can I see it today?

B Read the sentences. Correct the mistakes.

1. There *are* is no pets allowed in the building.

2. Are there a supermarket nearby?

3. How many bathrooms is there?

4. There isn't no bus stop near here.

5. Is there a lot of stores in the neighborhood?

6. There is three bedrooms.

7. There no a school near here.

8. Are there a dishwasher?

C You are looking for an apartment. Write questions that you would ask.

air-conditioning   bedrooms   bus stop   laundry room

park   parking   shops   traffic

1. _Is there air-conditioning?_

2. _____

3. _____

4. _____

5. _____

6. _____

7. _____

8. _____

D You have just looked at an apartment. Read your notes. Write sentences.

334 North Lincoln Street, Apt. 13

Good things about the apartment:
near bus stop
three bedrooms
laundry room in basement
no traffic on the street

Bad things about the apartment:
no parking
no air-conditioning
no shops nearby
no parks in the area

1. _There is no air-conditioning._

2. _____

3. _____

4. _____

5. _____

6. _____

7. _____

8. _____

A Listen and read.

FIVE TIPS FOR PROTECTING YOUR RIGHTS AS A RENTER

There are a lot of good reasons to rent a home. Sometimes, however, there can be problems. What if there's no heat? When should you get your security deposit back? Here are five tips to help you when renting.

Use online review sites

Look up your landlord or rental company. Have people complained about them? What problems have they
5 described. If a lot of people have left bad reviews, try to avoid that landlord or company.

Read your lease before you sign it

What fees or utilities are included? When can you get your deposit back? Do you have to pay for cleaning services before you leave?

Check your home for problems

10 Are all the appliances, such as your washer and dryer, working? Are there any leaks? Do the lights work? Make a list of any problems and get your landlord to fix them quickly. Depending on local rental laws, you may also be able to use part of your rent to pay for repairs.

Buy renters insurance

If your personal items are stolen or damaged, this will help cover the cost of replacing them.

15 *Make sure you get at least 30 days to move out*

Landlords may want you to move out without giving you a reason. In this case, they must write a letter with the date they need you to move out on. In some states, the landlord must let you know two months in advance.

B **DEVELOP YOUR ACADEMIC SKILLS.** Read the Academic Skill. Answer the questions.

1. What information would you learn from skimming this article?
   a. Tips for renters
   b. Why people rent
   c. Why it is better to rent than to buy

2. What should you read before signing?
   a. Your utility bills
   b. Local rental laws
   c. Your rental lease

3. What should you buy when living in a rented home?
   a. A new lease
   b. New lights
   c. Renters insurance

4. What is the least number of days you should be given to move out of your rented home?
   a. 1 day
   b. 30 days
   c. 90 days

> **Academic Skill: Skimming**
> Skimming means you do not read every word. Instead, you read quickly to get the general idea of the article.

C **CITE EVIDENCE.** Complete the sentences. Where is the information? Write the line number.

Lines

1. You should read _____ to find out what people have said about your landlord or rental company.
   a. online reviews
   b. your lease
   c. your insurance form   _____

2. Try to avoid landlords if _____.
   a. you can't pay the rent
   b. items in the house are broken
   c. they have a bad reputation   _____

3. You can find out what _____ are included in your rent by reading the lease.
   a. repairs
   b. fees and bills
   c. types of insurance   _____

4. When you move into a new home, make sure to _____.
   a. pay for cleaning services
   b. let your landlord know 60 days in advance
   c. check for any problems   _____

5. Depending on where you live, you can use _____ to pay for repairs.
   a. your lease
   b. renters insurance
   c. some of your rent   _____

D **WRITE ABOUT IT.** Have you ever had a problem renting a house or apartment? Describe what happened? How did you solve the problem?

_____

_____

_____

_____

_____

_____

A Look at the map and follow the directions. Where are you?
Write the name of each place.

1. Start at the hotel. Go west on Park Avenue. Turn right onto Main Street. The _____supermarket_____ is on the left.

2. Start at the restaurant. Go north on Main Street. At the supermarket, turn right onto School Road. Go through one traffic light. The _____ is on the left.

3. Start at the post office. Go south on Main Street. Go through two traffic lights. The _____ is on the right.

4. Start at the high school. Go south on Clark Street. At the toy store, turn right onto Park Avenue. The _____ is on the left.

5. Start at the shoe store. Go north on Main Street. Turn right onto Park Avenue. Go through one traffic light. At the next traffic light, turn left onto Clark Street. The _____ is on the left.

▶ **Listen. Circle the directions.**

1. a. At the traffic light, turn left.

    b. At the stop sign, turn right.

    c. At the stop sign, turn left.

2. a. Go straight.

    b. Turn right at this street.

    c. Go west on Fifth Street.

3. a. Go through two traffic lights.

    b. At the traffic light, turn left.

    c. Turn right at the pharmacy.

4. a. At the coffee shop, turn left.

    b. Go through two traffic lights.

    c. At the traffic light, turn right.

5. a. Go through one traffic light and turn left.

    b. At the stop sign, turn left.

    c. Turn left on Pine Street.

C ▶ **Listen. Complete the directions.**

Directions to the hospital:

Go straight on Miller Street.

_____ two traffic lights.

Turn _____ onto Ventura Avenue.

Go through three _____.

The hospital is on the _____.

Lesson 10: Writing

A Read the Writing Skill. Put the sentences in the correct order to make a paragraph. Write the numbers on the lines.

_____ **a.** My brother is trying to fix it, but he is very slow.

_____ **b.** It is leaking and I can't use it.

__1__ **c.** The sink in my apartment is not working.

_____ **d.** He is very helpful and can fix things quickly.

_____ **e.** I am calling the building manager later today.

> **Writing Skill: Structure paragraphs and use indents**
>
> The first line of a paragraph is indented. It begins a little bit in from the left. For example:
>
>   I like my apartment.
>
>   There are also some problems with the neighborhood.

B Write a paragraph. Use the sentences from Exercise A. Indent the first line.

_____

_____

_____

_____

_____

_____

C Read the text. Correct five errors.

My Apartment Search

I like my neighborhood. There are lots of nice apartments for rent. They are large and bright. Some are near the park and school. They all have bus stops nearby. Some of them has parking. The problem is that it cost a lot to live in this area. The rent does not include utilities. We can't spend a lot of money on rent because we are save to buy our own apartment in washington. We want to own our home. It is a good investment.

Lesson 11: Soft Skills at Work

A TAKE INITIATIVE. How can you take initiative at work? Check (✓) the correct answers.

❑ **a.** suggest improvements

❑ **b.** only do what you are asked

❑ **c.** help without being asked

Yusef is a cleaner
in an office building.
He works alone at night.

B Yusef calls Omar, his supervisor. Cross out the incorrect words. Then circle *True* or *False*.

1. Yusef: Hi, Omar. I **am / be** calling you with a question.

Omar: Of course. How can I help?

Yusef: There's no / There aren't any floor cleaner left. **Is there / Are there** another bottle?

Omar: Yes, **go / goes** down to the basement. There's a bottle on the top shelf.

Yusef: Thanks, Omar.

2. Yusef takes initiative.   True   False

C Omar calls Yusef at the end of his shift. Cross out the incorrect words. Then circle *True* or *False*.

1. Omar: Good morning, Yusef.

Yusef: Hello Omar. I am **finish up / finishing up** work now. I did the floors first. Then I cleaned the windows.

Omar: I didn't know they were dirty! Thanks. **Are there / Is there** anything else you need?

Yusef: No, I **am doing / is doing** fine now. Thanks.

2. Yusef only does what he was asked to do.   True   False

D JOB INFORMATION. Read the information. Then choose *True* or *False*.

Janitors and Building Cleaners
Janitors and building cleaners keep office buildings, schools, hospitals, retail stores, hotels, and other places clean, sanitary, and in good condition. Because office buildings often are cleaned while they are empty, many cleaners work evening hours.   Janitors and building cleaners often do the following: • Gather and empty trash.   • Sweep, mop, or vacuum building floors.   • Clean restrooms and stock them with supplies.

1. Janitors and cleaners keep the floors clean.   True   False

2. Janitors and cleaners only work in the evening.   True   False

Lesson 1: Vocabulary

A Complete the sentences.

| an anniversary party | a family reunion | a funeral | a graduation |
| a retirement party | a surprise party | ~~a wedding~~ | |

1. I'm going to ___*a wedding*___ on Saturday. My friends Arti and Ray are getting married.

2. Bob has worked at our company for 25 years. Today is his last day of work. We're having _____ for him at lunch.

3. Maxim and Olga are going to _____ today. It is their niece's last day of high school. Her whole family will be there to celebrate.

4. Lee and In-Ho Park got married on April 16, 1979. Today is April 16. Tonight they're having _____.

5. My grandparents are planning _____ this summer. All of my cousins, aunts, and uncles are going to be there.

6. Ted is 50 years old today. Ted doesn't know it, but his friends are having _____ for him.

7. Martin is going to _____ today. His Uncle Lucas died. He was 99 years old.

B ▶ Listen to the conversations. What kinds of events are the people attending?

1. _____

2. _____

3. _____

Lessons 2 & 3: Listening and Grammar

A Complete the paragraphs. Use the simple past.

Amy and Tom (stay) ___stayed___ at home on Saturday. Amy (bake) _____ cookies, and Tom (clean) _____ the kitchen. They both (wash) _____ the dishes. Tom (fix) _____ a leaking faucet, and Amy (paint) _____ the front door. They (work) _____ hard. In the evening, Amy and Tom (want) _____ to relax, so they (watch) _____ a movie on TV.

On Sunday, Amy (visit) _____ her friend. She (leave) _____ early in the morning. Tom (decide) _____ to stay at home. He (call) _____ his brother and (invite) _____ him for coffee at his house. He (show up) _____ at one o'clock. They (listen) _____ to some music and (talk) _____ all afternoon. Tom's brother (need) _____ to get up early the next day, so he (not stay) _____ very late.

B ▶ Listen. Complete the conversation.

Rich: How was the _____?

Ann: Very nice. We all missed you.

Rich: Yeah. I was sorry I couldn't go. Who was there?

Ann: The whole family _____ up. All the aunts, uncles, and cousins.

Rich: Aunt Lucy, too?

Ann: Of course. Everyone listened to her _____. And we looked at old photos and _____ of Grandma and Grandpa's wedding.

Rich: Oh yeah? I'm sorry I missed that!

Ann: Well, you should have come! We had a great time. We _____ and _____.

Rich: Really? I'll definitely have to go next time!

C Write sentences about the Park family's barbecue. What did the people do?
Use the past tense.

1. <u>In-Ho and Sun-Ah danced at the barbecue.</u>

2. _____

3. _____

4. _____

5. _____

6. _____

7. _____

D **WRITE ABOUT IT.** Describe an event that you attended with family or friends.
When was it? What did you do?

_____

_____

_____

Lesson 4: Workplace, Life, and Community Skills

A Read the descriptions and write the U.S. holidays.

Christmas Day	Columbus Day	Independence Day
Labor Day	Martin Luther King Jr. Day	Memorial Day
New Year's Day	Presidents' Day	Thanksgiving Day
Veterans Day		

1. On July 4, we celebrate the birthday of the United States.

_____

2. On the last Monday in May, we remember people who died in wars.

_____

3. On the third Monday in January, we remember the life of a great African-American leader.

_____

4. On January 1, we celebrate the first day of the year.

_____

5. On the first Monday in September, we have barbecues and say good-bye to summer.

_____

6. On October 13, we celebrate a man who sailed from Europe to North America.

_____

7. On the third Monday of February, we celebrate the birthdays of George Washington and Abraham Lincoln.

_____

8. On November 11, we honor people who served in the U.S. military.

_____

9. On the fourth Thursday of November, we get together with family to eat a large meal.

_____

10. On December 25, we decorate a tree and give gifts to family and friends.

_____

B Look at the calendar. Circle the dates for the holidays from Exercise A.

2019

JAN

S	M	T	W	T	F	S
	①	2	3	4	5	
6	7	8	9	10	11	12
13	14	15	16	17	18	19
20	21	22	23	24	25	26
27	28	29	30	31		

FEB

S	M	T	W	T	F	S
					1	2
3	④	5	6	7	8	9
10	11	12	13	14	15	16
17	18	19	20	21	22	23
24	25	26	27	28		

MAR

S	M	T	W	T	F	S
					1	2
3	4	5	6	7	8	9
10	11	12	13	14	15	16
17	18	19	20	21	22	23
24	25	26	27	28	29	30
31						

APR

S	M	T	W	T	F	S
	1	2	3	4	5	6
7	8	9	10	11	12	13
14	15	16	17	18	19	20
21	22	23	24	25	26	27
28	29	30				

MAY

S	M	T	W	T	F	S
			1	2	3	4
5	6	7	8	9	10	11
12	13	14	15	16	17	18
19	20	21	22	23	24	25
26	27	28	29	30	31	

JUN

S	M	T	W	T	F	S
						1
2	3	4	5	6	7	8
9	10	11	12	13	14	15
16	17	18	19	20	21	22
23	24	25	26	27	28	29
30						

JUL

S	M	T	W	T	F	S
	1	2	3	4	5	6
7	8	9	10	11	12	13
14	15	16	17	18	19	20
21	22	23	24	25	26	27
28	29	30	31			

AUG

S	M	T	W	T	F	S
				1	2	3
4	5	6	7	8	9	10
11	12	13	14	15	16	17
18	19	20	21	22	23	24
25	26	27	28	29	30	31

SEP

S	M	T	W	T	F	S
1	2	3	4	5	6	7
8	9	10	11	12	13	14
15	16	17	18	19	20	21
22	23	24	25	26	27	28
29	30					

OCT

S	M	T	W	T	F	S
	1	2	3	4	5	
6	7	8	9	10	11	12
13	14	15	16	17	18	19
20	21	22	23	24	25	26
27	28	29	30	31		

NOV

S	M	T	W	T	F	S
					1	2
3	4	5	6	7	8	9
10	11	12	13	14	15	16
17	18	19	20	21	22	23
24	25	26	27	28	29	30

DEC

S	M	T	W	T	F	S
1	2	3	4	5	6	7
8	9	10	11	12	13	14
15	16	17	18	19	20	21
22	23	24	25	26	27	28
29	30	31				

C **WRITE ABOUT IT.** Go online and find a holiday from another country that is celebrated in the U.S. When is it celebrated? Which country does it come from? What are the customs?

_____

_____

_____

Lessons 5 & 6: Listening and Grammar

A Use the past forms of the verbs.

1. Carlos **(go)** _____went_____ to school in Atlanta.

2. Melissa **(not get)** _____ a job at a bank.

3. Ahmed **(come)** _____ to New York in 2007.

4. Teresa **(make)** _____ good money working in a hospital.

5. Kate's parents **(grow)** _____ up in Lebanon.

6. I **(not take)** _____ any classes last year.

7. Roberto's parents **(get married)** _____ in the United States.

B Unscramble the questions. Then write short answers.

1. **A:** _Did you have a big wedding?_____
   (you / did / have / a big wedding)

   B: No, ___I didn't___. I had a small wedding.

2. **A:** _____
   (graduate / you / last year / did)

   B: Yes, _____. I graduated last December.

3. **A:** _____
   (did / get / a job / Anas / at a bank)

   B: No, _____. He got a job at a school.

4. **A:** _____
   (Lin / did / meet / in 2002 / her husband)

   B: Yes, _____. They met in January, 2002.

5. **A:** _____
   (a teacher / always / did / to be / want / Fatima)

   B: No, _____. She wanted to be a nurse.

6. **A:** _____
   (a small city / did / grow up / you / in)

   B: No, _____. I grew up in a big city.

Lesson 7: Reading

A ▶ Listen and read.

FIRST LADY MICHELLE OBAMA

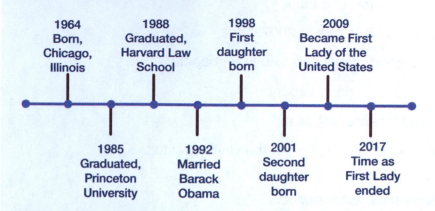

1964 Born, Chicago, Illinois	1988 Graduated, Harvard Law School	1998 First daughter born	2009 Became First Lady of the United States

1985 Graduated, Princeton University   1992 Married Barack Obama   2001 Second daughter born   2017 Time as First Lady ended

Michelle Obama is a writer and lawyer. She was the First Lady of the United States from 2009 to 2017. As First Lady, she helped with many important issues. She also inspired a lot of people.

Michelle Obama was born in Chicago in 1964. After high school, she went to Princeton University. She graduated in 1985. Then she went to Harvard Law School, graduating in 1988. After that, she worked in a law
5   firm in Chicago, where she met her husband, Barack Obama. They got married in 1992. They have two daughters. Malia was born in 1998, and Sasha was born in 2001.

Michelle Obama was the first African American to be the First Lady of the United States. As First Lady, she tried to help young people develop good eating habits and get more exercise. She talked a lot about healthy lifestyles. She also talked about the importance of education. She encouraged young people to work hard and
10   succeed. She once said, "I never cut class. I loved getting As. I liked being smart. I liked being on time. Being smart is cooler than anything in the world."

Michelle Obama was a good role model for girls and women. She became a woman who was admired by many people for many reasons.

B DEVELOP YOUR ACADEMIC SKILLS. Read the Academic Skill. Answer the questions.

What is Michelle Obama's older child called?
- **a.** Barack
- **b.** Malia
- **c.** Sasha

> **Academic Skill: Scan for information**
> Scanning an article means reading it quickly to find specific information, such as names and dates.

C IDENTIFY. What is the main idea of the article?

Michelle Obama _____.
- **a.** worked to inspire others
- **b.** liked being successful
- **c.** worked in a law firm

D CITE EVIDENCE. Complete the sentences. Where is the information? Write the line number.

Lines

1. After high school, Michelle Obama _____.
   a. got married
   b. became a lawyer
   c. attended a university   ____

2. In 2009, Michelle Obama became _____.
   a. a law student
   b. First Lady
   c. a great writer   ____

3. Michelle Obama encouraged young people to be _____.
   a. role models
   b. good students
   c. popular in school   ____

4. When she was First Lady, Michelle Obama _____.
   a. dressed well
   b. worked hard
   c. learned quickly   ____

E INTERPRET. Complete the sentences about the timeline.

1. Michelle Obama graduated from Harvard Law School when she was ____ years old.
   a. 14   **b.** 19   **c.** 24

2. When Michelle married Barack Obama, she was ____ years old.
   a. 26   **b.** 28   **c.** 30

3. Michelle Obama was First Lady of the United States for ____ years.
   a. 4   **b.** 6   **c.** 8

A Read the responses. Then write information questions.

1. **A:** (Why) _Why did you oversleep?_

   B: I overslept because I stayed up late last night.

2. **A:** (When) _____

   B: I had car trouble on Wednesday. My sister gave me a ride to work.

3. **A:** (Where) _____

   B: I found my wallet in my jacket pocket. I forgot to take it out.

4. **A:** (What) _____

   B: We went on a fishing trip last weekend. It rained the whole time!

5. **A:** (Why) _____

   B: I took the wrong bus because I didn't have a bus map.

6. **A:** (What time) _____

   B: I left work at 7:30 last night. I was really busy.

B ▶ Listen. Answer the questions with complete sentences.

1. Why did Jason oversleep? _____

2. What did Jason forget first on his way to work? _____

3. What bus did Jason take? _____

4. What time did Jason get to work? _____

5. Where did Jason try to buy lunch? _____

C Look at the pictures. The Carlson family took a trip last year. What problems did they have?

1. _The Carlson family got stuck in traffic._

2. _____

3. _____

4. _____

5. _____

D WRITE ABOUT IT. Have you ever had problems on a vacation? What happened? How did you feel?

_____

_____

_____

Lesson 10: Writing

A Read the Writing Skill. Which sentences need a comma? Check (✓) the boxes.

> **Writing Skill: Use commas with dates**
> When you begin a sentence with a date, add a comma. For example:
>
> In 2016, my daughter graduated from high school.
>
> When you end a sentence with a date, do not add a comma. For example:
>
> My daughter started college in 2017.

❑ **a.** I play piano well. I took my first lesson in the summer of 1997.

❑ **b.** In 1995 we moved to a new neighborhood in San Diego.

❑ **c.** My sister lives in China. I have not seen her since 2014.

❑ **d.** The whole family came back for Uncle David's funeral in 1988.

❑ **e.** In 1985 my son was born.

B Rewrite each sentence. Move the date to begin or end the sentence. Add or delete a comma.

1. Maria started teaching in 2011.   _In 2011, Maria started teaching._

2. Chen moved to the city in 1934.   _____

3. In 2015, we visited my family.   _____

4. Alex got his first bike in 1984.   _____

5. Mona got a new job in 1993.   _____

C Read the text. Circle four more errors.

Rohan was born in Mumbai, in 1972. He grow up in India but moved to the U.S. to study. In 1995, he graduates from medical school. He worked in a hospital in New York, until 2003. Now he works as a doctor in a health center in chicago.

Lesson 11: Soft Skills at Work

A **BE DEPENDABLE.** How can you be dependable at work? Check (✓) the correct answers.

❑ **a.** arrive at work on time

❑ **b.** always finish a job

❑ **c.** leave early for lunch

❑ **d.** call if you are going to be late

Chunhua works at a hospital. She is a nurse.

B A co-worker asks Chunhua for help. Cross out the incorrect words. Then complete the sentence.

1. Chunhua: You asked to see me, Dr. Cruz?

Dr. Cruz: Yes, can you help **I / me** with something, please?

Chunhua: Of course. I **will be / won't be** free in 10 minutes.

Dr. Cruz: Oh, I want to get **start / started** right away.

Chunhua: I'm sorry. I need to finish these charts **of / for** Dr. Lin first.

2. Chunhua is dependable because she _____.

a. comes to work on time

b. finishes her job

c. agrees to help

C Chunhua asks a co-worker for help. Cross out the incorrect words. Then circle *True* or *False*.

1. Chunhua: Hi, Martin. Can you cover my shift on Tuesday?

Martin: Tuesday? Well, I **do / don't** have any plans yet.

Chunhua: Okay. So you can work on **this / that** day for me?

Martin: I don't know. I might go to the beach. Can I text you on Tuesday morning?

Chunhua: That's okay. I'll ask someone **other / else**.

2. Martin is dependable.   True   False

Lesson 1: Vocabulary

A Match the health problem with the pictures.

a.

b.

c.

d.

e.

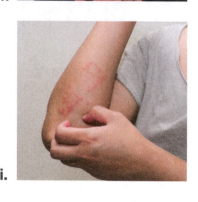
f.

g.

h.

i.

1. __a__ the flu
2. _____ a cold
3. _____ a cough

4. _____ an earache
5. _____ a headache
6. _____ heartburn

7. _____ a sore throat
8. _____ a rash
9. _____ an upset stomach

B Cross out the incorrect words.

1. Lan feels hot. She has **a** / ~~the~~ fever.

2. I feel cold and then hot. I have **a** / **the** flu.

3. Rod can't eat. He has **a** / **an** upset stomach.

4. Jon needs to lie down. He has **a** / **the** headache.

5. Call a doctor, now! Mr. Pardo has **the** / **(no word)** chest pains.

6. My arm is red! I have **a** / **(no word)** rash.

7. No onions, please. Onions give me **a** / **(no word)** heartburn.

8. Ms. Wilson does not eat salty foods. She has **a** / **(no word)** high blood pressure.

9. My brother can't talk today. He has **a** / **an** sore throat.

10. The baby sounds very sick. He has **a** / **the** cough.

C ▶ Listen. Complete the email.

Dear Grandma,

We are on vacation this week. Last weekend, we went camping at a state park. We did NOT have a good time. Dad cooked on the campfire every night. The food was really bad. Dad had _____heartburn_____, and I had _____. On Saturday, it rained all day. Mom got sick. She had _____ and _____. On Sunday, Janet and I went swimming. Janet got water in her ear. Now she has _____. Then Dad and I went hiking. Now I have _____ on my arms and legs. This morning we went to a hotel. No more camping for us!

Love,
Marie

A Cross out the incorrect words.

Receptionist: Good morning, Dr. Solano's office.

Carmen: Hi, this is Carmen Pinto. I have an appointment **on** / ~~in~~ Wednesday morning.

Receptionist: Yes, Mrs. Pinto. Your appointment is **at** / **in** 10:30.

Carmen: I need to change it to Wednesday afternoon.

Receptionist: I'm sorry. Our office closes **on** / **at** 1:00 **on** / **in** Wednesdays.

Carmen: How about this afternoon?

Receptionist: Well, we're closed for lunch **at** / **from** 12:00 **to** / **by** 1:00. But I have an opening **from** / **in** an hour.

Carmen: That's great. I'll see you then.

B Read the text message. Answer the questions using complete sentences.

1. What day of the week is the patient's appointment?

   The appointment is on Thursday.

2. What is the date of the appointment?

   _____

3. When does the clinic open on Mondays?

   _____

4. What time does the clinic close on Saturdays?

   _____

5. Imagine it is now 3:20 P.M. on November 19.
   How soon is the patient's appointment?

   _____

6. The patient has never been to the clinic before.
   What time should he arrive?

   _____

> ●●○○ 🔋   **3:57 PM**   %33 🔋
>
> Hi, Evan. You have an appointment with Dr. Bernard on Thursday, November 19 at 03:45 P.M. at Downtown Health Clinic, 10 Central Street, Newtown, KS. Reply "Y" to confirm your appointment. As a new patient, please arrive 20 minutes before your appointment time.
>
> Call (313) 555-1234 to reschedule. Office hours: M-F 7:00 A.M.-7:00 P.M., Sat 8:00 A.M.-6:00 P.M.

Lesson 4: Workplace, Life, and Community Skills

A Match the definitions with the words.

dosage	expiration date	over-the-counter (OTC) medicine
~~patient~~	prescription	refill

1. The person who sees a doctor for medical help   _____ *patient* _____

2. The date you should throw away medicine   _____

3. Medicine you can buy without an order from a doctor   _____

4. An order for medicine from a doctor   _____

5. The amount of medicine you take and when you take it   _____

6. The number of times you can get more medicine   _____

B Read the medicine label. Then circle *True* or *False*.

1. Take this medicine for a headache.

   True   (False)

2. Take 2 tablets every hour.

   True   False

3. Don't take more than 2 tablets in one day.

   True   False

4. Children age 12 and older can take this medicine.

   True   False

5. You must not use this medicine after January 2020.

   True   False

BioMed Pharmacy

Active Ingredient: Calcium Carbonate USP 1,000 mg

Uses: Relieves heartburn and upset stomach

Directions:
- Take 2 tablets every hour, as needed.

Warnings:
- Do not take more than 8 tablets in 24 hours.
- If you are taking a prescription medicine, ask your doctor before taking this product.
- Not for children under 12.
- Keep out of reach of children.

Expiration date: 01/2020

C Read the prescription label. Answer the questions.

1. Who is this prescription for? _____Sarah Carlton_____
2. What part of the body is the medicine for? _____
3. How much medicine does Sarah take? _____
4. How often does she take the medicine? _____
5. How many refills can she get? _____
6. What is the expiration date? _____

GREENVILLE DRUGSTORE
Doctor: Alfred Finley, MD
Patient: Sarah Carlton
Dosage: Put four drops in each eye every 4 to 6 hours for four days.
Warning: For the eyes only. Do not use with children under 12.
Polymazin B
No refills
Expiration date: 3/25/2021

D ▶ Listen. Complete the conversation.

Pharmacist: Mr. Bronson, your prescription is ready. Is this the first time you are taking Naproxen?

Mr. Bronson: Yes, it is. How much do I take?

Pharmacist: Take _____ tablets _____ a day.

Mr. Bronson: Do I take them with _____?

Pharmacist: Yes. Take the tablets at breakfast, lunch, and dinner.

Mr. Bronson: And how long do I take them?

Pharmacist: _____.

Mr. Bronson: All right.

Pharmacist: This medicine can make you feel _____ or nauseous. If this happens, stop taking the medicine and call your _____.

Mr. Bronson: OK.

Pharmacist: Do you understand these _____?

Mr. Bronson: Yes, I do. Thank you.

E WRITE ABOUT IT. Search for an online pharmacy. On the website, find information for a medicine to treat headaches. How often can you take it? How many can you take in a day? Is it suitable for children?

_____

_____

_____

Lessons 5 & 6: Listening and Grammar

A Complete the sentences. Use the past tense of the words.

fall	~~have~~	sprain

1. Maria ___*had*___ a bad accident in her house. She _____ down the stairs, and she _____ her arm.

break	get	go

2. Andrew _____ hurt at work. He _____ his ankle, and he _____ to the emergency room.

get	have	take

3. Fang _____ sick last week. She _____ the flu. I _____ her to the doctor.

cut	have	not go

4. The new cook _____ an accident yesterday. She _____ her hand with a knife, but she _____ to hospital.

have	get	go

5. Lee _____ a bad fever last week. He _____ to the doctor, and _____ some medicine at the pharmacy.

B WRITE ABOUT IT. Describe a time when you or someone you know got hurt. What happened?

My sister broke her arm when she was 11 years old.
She fell from a tree.

_____

_____

_____

_____

_____

A DEVELOP YOUR ACADEMIC SKILLS. Read the Academic Skill. Look at the formatting in the text before you read the article. Circle the main point of the second paragraph.

a. Technology helps us measure our health.
b. Technology helps us be more active.
c. We do not need technology to track our health.

> **Academic Skill: Use formatting clues**
> Authors sometimes use formatting such as **boldface** type, bullets (•), and color to help readers find the main point.

B ▶ Listen and read.

HEALTH AND TECHNOLOGY

Technology can help us keep fit, but it can also harm our health.

A HELPFUL TOOL

Keeping track We need three simple things for
5 good health. We must eat well, sleep well, and exercise. However, sometimes it is hard to keep track of how we are doing. This is why many people use activity trackers. This technology measures our exercise and sleep. It tells us how
10 many steps we take or how far we run. It also tells us how strong and healthy our heart is.

Better habits We can use the information we get from activity trackers to change our habits. For example, we can exercise more and go to bed earlier. This will help our health.

15 **HARMFUL EFFECTS**

Always "on" Technology is not always good for us. People use smartphones, tablets, and computers all day long. This means people are always "on." They do not take time to relax.

Memory loss Too much technology makes us forget things. We do not remember facts. We know we can look them up online.

20 **Poor sleep** Just 50 years ago, people got 8.5 hours of sleep a night. Adults now get less than seven hours of sleep a night. One of the reasons for this is that we are spending more time on social media. We often check phones and tablets in bed, and the light from screens makes it difficult for us to sleep.

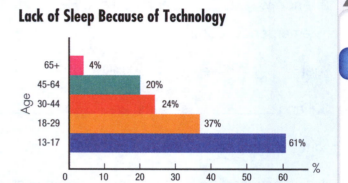

Lack of Sleep Because of Technology

Age	%
65+	4%
45-64	20%
30-44	24%
18-29	37%
13-17	61%

Note: percentage of people that sleep less than seven hours in each age group because of their use of technology in bed.

C IDENTIFY. What is the main idea of the article?

a. Technology is good for health.
b. Technology is bad for health.
c. Technology affects health in different ways.

D CITE EVIDENCE. **Complete the sentences. Where is the information? Write the line number.**

Lines

1. The key to good health is _____.
   a. using technology
   b. taking time to relax
   c. exercise, sleep, and healthy food   _____

2. An activity tracker can _____.
   a. show us what we need to change
   b. improve our sleep
   c. improve our memory   _____

3. A person who is always "on" _____.
   a. can feel stress
   b. is good at relaxing
   c. is good at using computers   _____

4. Technology _____ because it makes us lazy.
   a. damages our sleep
   b. reduces our memory
   c. reduces our exercise   _____

E INTERPRET. **Complete the sentences about the chart.**

1. Technology most affects the sleep of _____.
   a. adults   **b.** the youngest age group   **c.** the oldest age group

2. Only one group's percentage of bad sleep is _____.
   a. lower than 5%   **b.** lower than 10%   **c.** higher than 10%

3. The percentage of bad sleep among people aged 45-64 is _____ that among people aged 30-44.
   a. the same as   **b.** higher than   **c.** lower than

4. The percentage of bad sleep among people aged 18-29 is _____ higher than that among people aged 30-44.
   a. 24%   **b.** 16%   **c.** 13%

A Cross out the incorrect words.

1. Hector took some cold medicine **for / because** he had the flu.

2. Edgar has bad heartburn. He went to the doctor **for / because** a prescription.

3. Ren had a headache. He went to the drugstore **for / because** some pain reliever.

4. Aunt Rita's foot is swollen **for / because** she fell in the bathtub. She needs to buy a rubber safety mat.

5. Mrs. Woo needs new glasses. She called her eye doctor **for / because** an appointment.

6. I need to call my boss. I can't go to work today **for / because** I hurt my ankle.

B Complete the sentences. Write *because* or *for*.

1. My daughter didn't go to school today ___because___ she didn't feel well. I went to the drugstore _____ some flu medicine.

2. Eva took her baby to the clinic _____ she had a fever. The doctor asked her to come back next week _____ a blood test.

3. I went to the dental clinic _____ I needed a checkup. I had to wait a long time _____ they were very busy.

4. I went to the doctor _____ a flu shot. I wanted to get the shot _____ I had the flu last year and I missed a lot of work.

5. Camila always misses class. Last week she was absent _____ she had a sore throat. Today she's absent _____ she has to work.

C Look at the pictures. Answer the questions. There may be more than one correct answer.

1. Why did Roberto go to the drugstore?

(because) _He went to the drugstore because_ _he needed eye drops._

(for) _____

_____

Roberto

2. Why did Sharon miss work?

(because) _____

_____

Sharon

3. Why did Haseem call 911?

(because) _____

_____

Haseem

4. Why did Isabel go to the doctor?

(because) _____

_____

(for) _____

_____

FLU SHOTS TODAY

Isabel

5. Why did Anton call his supervisor?

(because) _____

_____

Anton

Lesson 10: Writing

A Read the Writing Skill. Then circle the reasons.

1. (Maha's son has a rash). She puts cream on his leg
   three times a day.

2. I take the medicine at 6:30 in the morning. I need to have
   it one hour before breakfast.

3. Mr. Kumar walks to work every morning. He needs to exercise.

4. Martin has a bad cold. He makes a hot drink with lemon and honey.

Writing Skill : Give a reason

Give a reason why you do something. For example:

When I have a headache, I lie down. (It helps me feel better.)

B Look at the pictures. Add reasons to the sentences.

1. Tam has to stay in bed today
   because she has a fever.

2. Nick is going to be late for his
   doctor's appointment
   _____.

3. Carlos can't go swimming for six
   weeks
   _____.

4. Olga is not going to give a
   presentation today
   _____.

C Read the text. Correct four more errors.

When I ~~has~~ *have* the flu, I don't go to class. I stay home for I don't want to make

other people sick. I rest in bed in morning to evening. I also take a pain

reliever because the fever. I are usually better by the next day.

Lesson 11: Soft Skills at Work

A RESPECT OTHERS AT WORK. How can you respect others at work? Check (✓) the correct answers.

❑ **a.** do your share of the work

❑ **b.** think about what other people need or feel

❑ **c.** buy coffee for your manager

Belvie works at a factory.

B Belvie meets a co-worker in the staff kitchen. Cross out the incorrect words. Then circle *True* or *False*.

1. Belvie: Hi, Maria. How are you?

   Maria: Not good. I **have / had** a sore throat last night.

   Belvie: Oh! Do you feel better now?

   Maria: Yes, I took medicine **for / because** it. I'm just tired. My shift starts **on / in**

        ten minutes. I need some coffee!

   Belvie: OK! Let me wash my cup first.

2. Belvie respects her co-workers.   **True**   **False**

C Belvie talks with another co-worker. Cross out the incorrect words. Then circle *True* or *False*.

1. Belvie: The radio was a bit loud this morning. Could you turn it down **in / at** the afternoon?

   Ali: Sure. I thought you liked listening to it.

   Belvie: I usually do, but I **have / had** a headache earlier. The music made my head

        hurt / hurting more.

   Ali: Sorry to hear that. I'll turn it off.

2. Ali respects others at work.   **True**   **False**

D JOB INFORMATION. Read the information. Then choose *True* or *False*.

Sick Leave
Sick leave is time off from work when you are sick. There are two kinds of sick leave: paid and unpaid. There are no federal laws that say employers have to give employees paid sick leave. There are laws that say that some companies have to give unpaid sick leave. Many states have additional laws about paid and unpaid sick leave.

1. Federal laws say that all employees should get paid sick leave.   **True**   **False**

2. Many states also have laws about sick leave.   **True**   **False**

Lesson 1: Vocabulary

A Match the words to form a job duty.

1. prepare   _d_
2. stock   ___
3. install   ___
4. unload   ___
5. record   ___
6. supervise   ___

a. computer systems
b. patient information
c. employees
~~d.~~ food
e. shelves
f. materials

B Look at the pictures. Write the job duty. Use job duties from Exercise A.

1. ___prepare food___

2. _____

3. _____

4. _____

5. _____

6. _____

C Look at the pictures. Write the job title and two job duties for each picture. There may be more than one correct answer.

1. Job title: _food service worker_

Job duties: _prepare food, clean_
kitchen equipment

2. Job title: _____

Job duties: _____

_____

3. Job title: _____

Job duties: _____

_____

4. Job title: _____

Job duties: _____

_____

B **WRITE ABOUT IT.** Think of three people you know. Write their job titles and duties.

Blanca is a stock clerk. She stocks shelves and assists customers.

_____

_____

_____

Lessons 2 & 3: Listening and Grammar

A Complete the sentences. Use *can* or *can't* and a verb from the box.

lift	operate	order	speak
prepare	~~type~~	use	

1. Nada uses a computer a lot. She _____*can type*_____ about 44 words per minute.

2. Lola doesn't know how to drive. She _____ a forklift.

3. Trung only speaks Vietnamese and English. He _____ Spanish.

4. Delma doesn't know how to use a computer. She _____ a word-processing program.

5. Salman is a cook at a restaurant. She _____ food.

6. Chen knows what we need for the office. He _____ supplies.

7. Edgar isn't very strong. He _____ boxes over 35 pounds.

B Read the answers. Write *Yes / No* questions with *can*.

1. **A:** _Can you lift heavy boxes?_____

    B: No, I can't. I can't lift heavy boxes. I hurt my back.

2. **A:** _____

    B: Yes, she can. Ms. Navarro can speak English well.

3. **A:** _____

    B: Yes, he can. Diego can order more spaghetti for the kitchen.

4. **A:** _____

    B: No, I can't. I don't know how to type. But I can learn.

5. **A:** _____

    B: No, he can't. David can't work on Sundays.

C Imagine you are the manager of a supermarket. You need a new stock clerk, cashier, and food service worker. You need to interview job applicants for each position. Write three questions you can ask the applicants.

stock clerk

Can you lift heavy boxes?

_____

_____

cashier

_____

_____

_____

food service worker

_____

_____

_____

D Look at the applicants and their skills. Choose one person for each supermarket job in Exercise C. Explain your choices.

Applicants	Skills						
	use a cash register	lift heavy boxes	stock shelves	operate a forklift	order supplies	prepare food	clean kitchen equipment
Igor		✓	✓	✓	✓		
Marie	✓		✓		✓		
Chan		✓			✓	✓	✓

I'm going to give Igor the stock clerk job because. . .

_____

_____

_____

Lesson 4: Workplace, Life, and Community Skills

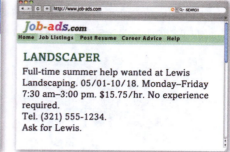

OFFICE ASSISTANT

Full-time office assistant position available. Computer skills required. Three years' office experience preferred.
Health insurance and vacation included.
Email résumé to hr@modelagency.com.
No calls please.

Night Shift Manager

Full-time position available in paper warehouse. Night shift (10 pm-7 am). Full benefits and vacation after three months. Four years' experience supervising employees required. Apply in person only Monday–Friday 1 pm–5 pm. 325 Lincoln Street.
Bring references.

LANDSCAPER

Full-time summer help wanted at Lewis Landscaping. 05/01-10/18. Monday–Friday 7:30 am–3:00 pm. $15.75/hr. No experience required.
Tel. (321) 555-1234.
Ask for Lewis.

A Read the help-wanted ads. Then read the statements. Circle *True* or *False*.

1. The office assistant job is part-time.   True   (False)

2. You need computer skills for the office assistant job.   True   False

3. You call the company to apply for the office assistant job.   True   False

4. The night manager shift is from 1:00 P.M. to 5:00 P.M.   True   False

5. You get benefits after three months at the night manager job.   True   False

6. You go to 325 Lincoln Street to apply for the manager job.   True   False

7. The landscaper job is from May to October only.   True   False

8. You need experience for the landscaper job.   True   False

B Read about Gilbert Reyes. Then look at the help-wanted ads in Exercise A. Which job is the best match for Gilbert? Explain your answer.

Gilbert Reyes is looking for a job. In Puerto Rico, he was the assistant manager in an office for four years where he helped organize work schedules. He needs to work full-time. He likes working in an office. He needs a job with health benefits because he has a wife and a six-year-old son. Gilbert can supervise employees, use a computer, and type fast. He has good references from his old job in Puerto Rico.

_____

_____

_____

C WRITE ABOUT IT. Search for a job posting website. What job are you interested in? Write about the skills and experience you have for this job.

_____

_____

_____

Lessons 5 & 6: Listening and Grammar

A Complete the sentences. Write *ago*, *in*, or *later*.

David Ho was born in Taiwan **(1.)** ___in___ 1952. His father went to the United States to work. Nine years **(2.)** _____, Mr. Ho brought his wife and two sons to the U.S. when David was twelve years old. The family lived in Los Angeles. David went to school, but he didn't understand English. He studied very hard. He learned English **(3.)** _____ six months. David went to college and studied medicine. He became a doctor. **(4.)** _____ the 1990s, he studied a terrible new disease called AIDS. Dr. Ho made medicine for people who had AIDS. **(5.)** _____ 1996, Dr. Ho received *Time Magazine*'s "Man of the Year" award. Now people with AIDS can live longer than they did 20 years **(6.)** _____.

B ▶ Listen to stories about two immigrants to the U.S. Complete the time lines. Write the dates and milestones.

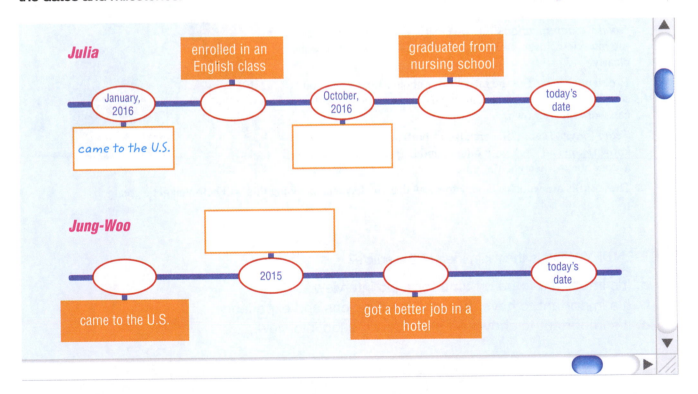

 **DEVELOP YOUR ACADEMIC SKILLS.** Read the Academic Skill. Look at the title and pictures in the text. Circle the correct answer.

The topic of the text will be _____.
- **a.** job interviews
- **b.** social events
- **c.** celebrations

> **Academic Skill: Predict the topic**
> You can often guess what an article is about by looking at the title and pictures. This will prepare you to understand what you read.

B ▶ Listen and read.

KEY TO GETTING A GOOD JOB

How do you get the job of your dreams? You need to have the right skills. This means having the qualifications, experience, and ability to do the job.

You need to have some other skills as well. These are sometimes called "soft skills." These skills are about what you are like as a
5 person, how you do things, and how you get along with other people. During a job interview, you must show that you have these skills.

Here are some soft skills that employers look for in employees.

Enthusiasm Show enthusiasm by being on time, asking questions,
10 and listening. Employers like people who have enthusiasm.

Good Communication Can you clearly explain your ideas? In a job interview, make sure you answer questions confidently and clearly.

Problem Solving Tell the interviewer about a time when you
15 solved a difficult problem. Employers also want to know if you can work on your own.

Team Player Team skills are also important. Employers want to know if you can work with others, and help and guide them. Tell a story about when you did this.

20 These skills are valuable, so try to show that you have them. Doing this will help you get a great job.

C **IDENTIFY.** What is the main idea of the article?

- **a.** It's important to be on time for a job interview.
- **b.** It's important to have the right qualifications and experience.
- **c.** It's important to show soft skills during a job interview.

D CITE EVIDENCE. Complete the sentences. Where is the information? Write the line number.

Lines

1. Soft skills are skills you use to _____.
   a. solve math problems
   b. fix computer systems
   c. communicate with others   _____

2. Good communication means being able to _____.
   a. hide your feelings
   b. talk about your ideas
   c. change your opinions   _____

3. Employers prefer employees who can _____.
   a. handle problems
   b. create work
   c. ignore complaints   _____

4. Being a team player is about _____.
   a. talking a lot
   b. guiding others
   c. selling items   _____

5. You can demonstrate your soft skills by _____.
   a. talking about when you used them
   b. shaking hands with the interviewer
   c. being on time for the interview   _____

E WRITE ABOUT IT. Think about a job interview you or someone you know had. Answer the questions.

1. Did you/they show enthusiasm? How?

_____

2. Did you/they demonstrate your/their problem-solving skills? How?

_____

3. Did you/they demonstrate being a team player?

_____

4. What other soft skills are important to show during a job interview?

_____

Lessons 8 & 9: Listening and Grammar

A Complete the conversations. Write *and* or *or*.

1. **A:** What's your availability?

   B: I can work weekdays ___and___ weekends. I need all the hours you can give me.

2. **A:** Can you work Monday through Friday?

   B: No, I can't work on Tuesdays _____ Thursdays. I have classes on those days.

3. **A:** Does your class meet twice a week?

   B: Yes, we meet on Monday _____ Wednesday mornings.

4. **A:** Do you have transportation to work?

   B: Yes, I do. I can take the bus _____ get a ride from my husband.

5. **A:** Do you prefer first shift _____ second shift?

   B: I prefer first shift. I have an English class at night. But I'm flexible.

B ▶ Listen. Answer the interview questions. Check (✓) the boxes.

1. When can you work?
   - ☐ Saturday
   - ☐ Sunday

2. When can you work?
   - ☐ first shift
   - ☐ second shift

3. When can you work?
   - ☐ breakfast shift
   - ☐ lunch shift
   - ☐ dinner shift

4. When can you work?
   - ☐ weekdays
   - ☐ weekends
   - ☐ days
   - ☐ evenings

C Imagine you are the manager at a café. Read about your employees' availability. Then complete the schedule. Choose one employee for each shift. Each employee must work at least 20 hours.

Rosa

I can work mornings and afternoons. I can't work on Wednesday or Friday mornings because I have a class. I can't work on weekends.

Fang

I can't work on Fridays or Saturday mornings. I prefer to work the afternoon shift.

Paul

I can't work on Tuesdays or Thursdays. I can work on weekends. I prefer to work mornings.

Coffee Stop Café	Employee Schedule		April 7 – April 13				
	Mon.	Tue.	Wed.	Thu.	Fri.	Sat.	Sun.
Morning Shift 6:30 – 11:30 a.m.							
Afternoon Shift 11:00 a.m. – 4:00 p.m.							

D WRITE ABOUT IT. Imagine you are looking for a job. Complete the job application about your work availability

When can you work? Check (✓) the boxes.

❑ Mon. ❑ Tues. ❑ Wed. ❑ Thurs. ❑ Fri. ❑ Sat. ❑ Sun.

❑ mornings ❑ afternoons ❑ evenings

Lesson 10: Writing

A Read the skill. Cross out the incorrect words.

1. In 2017, I **was / ~~am~~** a landscaper.

2. Now, I **owned / own** my own business.

3. After college, I **became / become** a nurse.

4. Today, I **was / am** a doctor in Memphis.

5. Last year, I **joined / join** the sales team.

> **Writing Skill: Use the correct tense**
>
> Use the simple past to explain your previous jobs. Use the present tense to explain your current job. For example:
>
> Past: I (was) a cook in New York.
>
> Present: Now, I (am) a hotel manager in San Francisco.

B Complete the paragraph. Use the present or simple past form of the words.

I ___worked___ (work) in many jobs. In 2016, I _____ (start) working as a food service worker. I _____ (clean) kitchen equipment most of the day. After two years, I _____ (become) a manager. I _____ (manage) a large team. However, I _____ (am) ready for a change. Today, I _____ (begin) my night classes.

C Read the text. Correct five more errors.

In 2015, I ~~work~~ *worked* in an electronic store in California. I stocked shelves, help customers, and answered their questions. In 2016, I go to San Jose and worked in a car factory. Last years, I move to Florida and started working in a hotel. I can't wait to started another job soon.

Lesson 11: Soft Skills at Work

A **HONESTY AT WORK.** How can you be honest at work? Check (✓) the correct answers.

❏ **a.** be truthful to co-workers

❏ **b.** admit when you make a mistake

❏ **c.** work extra hours

❏ **d.** refuse to lie to others

❏ **e.** keep accurate records

Rodrigo is going to interviews. He is looking for a new job.

B Rodrigo is at an interview. Cross out the incorrect words. Then circle *True* or *False*.

1. Interviewer: Why did you leave your first job?

    Rodrigo: I **can / can't** explain. I was there for three years and I wanted a change.

    Interviewer: A year **last / later**, you changed jobs again.

    Rodrigo: Yes, that's right.

    Interviewer: Were you bored again **and / or** was there another reason?

    Rodrigo: No, I wasn't bored at that job. However, the salary was very low.

2. Rodrigo is honest.   **True**   **False**

C Rodrigo is at another interview. Cross out the incorrect words. Then answer the question.

1. Interviewer: Tell me about your **last / ago** job.

    Rodrigo: I worked as a gardener.

    Interviewer: Did you like that job?

    Rodrigo: Yes. I **can / can't** work outside **and / or** I've always liked growing flowers.

    Interviewer: That can be hard work. Did you ever make any mistakes?

    Rodrigo: Yes, I did sometimes. But I always fixed them

2. In what way is Rodrigo honest?

    a. He never makes mistakes.

    b. He likes working outside.

    c. He says that he sometimes made mistakes.

Unit 9: Parents and Children

Lesson 1: Vocabulary

A Look at the pictures. Write the school subjects. Use the words from the box.

art	community service	language arts/English		math
music	~~P.E. (physical education)~~	science	social studies/history	technology

1. P.E. (physical education)

2. ______________________

3. ______________________

4. ______________________

5. ______________________

6. ______________________

7. ______________________

8. ______________________

9. ______________________

B Write each student's favorite subject. Use subjects from Exercise A.

My favorite subject is
_____.
I like to paint with finger paint and color pictures.

1.

My favorite subject is _____.
I learned all the names of the presidents.

2.

My favorite subject is _____.
I love numbers. I learned how to add and subtract numbers.

3.

My favorite subject is _____.
My dream is to design my own robot in the future.

4.

C Read the descriptions of classes in the high school course catalog. Write the title of each course with a school subject from Exercise A.

Greenville High School
Grade 9 Course List

Greenville High School

1. **Course:** _____ *music* _____
   Students will learn how to read music notes and play one of these instruments: piano, drums, violin, or clarinet.

2. **Course:** _____
   Students will learn how to play team sports (soccer or volleyball) and individual sports (swimming or running).

3. **Course:** _____
   Students will work 30 hours with an organization that helps people. Students will help at a food bank, teach younger children, or clean around lakes and rivers.

4. **Course:** _____
   Students will read and write stories, learn grammar, and discuss literature.

5. **Course:** _____
   Students will learn basic computer skills, such as using the internet and using word processing programs.

Lessons 2 & 3: Listening and Grammar

A Complete the conversations using *will* for the future.

1. **A:** Ben (not have) _____won't have_____ school next Thursday. There's a parent-teacher conference that day.

    B: I know. My mother (watch) _____ the kids that day.

2. **A:** My daughter (be) _____ in the school play in December.

    B: How exciting! I (plan) _____ to go.

3. **A:** The next PTO meeting (be) _____ on January 17.

    B: Oh no! I (not be) _____ there. I have to babysit my niece.

4. **A:** My soccer team (play) _____ in a big game on Friday. Can you come?

    B: Well, I have to work that night, but I (try) _____ to change my schedule.

B ▶ Listen. Complete the announcement.

Good morning, students. We have a busy week at Greenville Middle School. The Music Club _____ a bake sale today. Club members _____ cookies and other baked goods from 11:30 to 12:30 in the cafeteria. The Technology Club _____ in the library today at 4:00. Bad news, Greenville basketball fans. There _____ a basketball game on Wednesday. The Greenville Tigers _____ their next home game on Monday at 7:00 P.M. Don't forget there _____ a Back-to-school Night for parents on Thursday at 7:30. Your parents _____ your classes and meet your teachers . . . but they _____ your homework for you! And finally, on Friday, the seventh grade class _____ a field trip to the Greenville Science Museum. Please remember to bring a bag lunch. Thank you and have a good day.

Lesson 4: Workplace, Life, and Community Skills

A ▶ Listen. Complete the phone message.

Date: _February 5th_

To: _____

From: _____

Phone: _____

Message: _____

_____

B Read the voicemail message. Circle *True* or *False*.

1. The message is from Alba's teacher.

   True   False

2. Alba plays sports after school on Wednesday.

   True   False

3. Alba can take the test on Wednesday.

   True   False

4. Mr. Rivas works a night shift.

   True   False

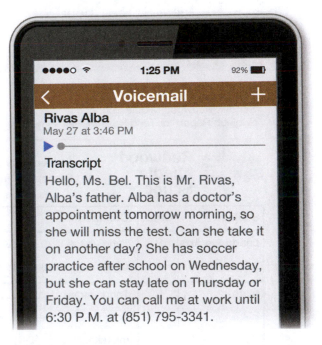

●●●●○ 📶   1:25 PM   92% 🔋

< **Voicemail** +

Rivas Alba
May 27 at 3:46 PM

▶ ●────────────

Transcript
Hello, Ms. Bel. This is Mr. Rivas, Alba's father. Alba has a doctor's appointment tomorrow morning, so she will miss the test. Can she take it on another day? She has soccer practice after school on Wednesday, but she can stay late on Thursday or Friday. You can call me at work until 6:30 P.M. at (851) 795-3341.

C WRITE ABOUT IT. What would you say in your personal voicemail greeting? Write full sentences.

_____

_____

_____

Lessons 5 & 6: Listening and Grammar

A Cross out the incorrect words.

1. Maya is a **good** / ~~well~~ writer. Her book report was excellent.

2. Finn didn't pass his math test because he didn't work **careful** / **carefully**.

3. Bo got a 97 on his math exam. He studied **hard** / **hardly**.

4. It is difficult to read Pablo's papers. He doesn't write **neat** / **neatly**.

5. Anita finished her homework in half an hour. She worked **quick** / **quickly**.

6. My daughter is having trouble in science. She is a **poor** / **poorly** student in that subject.

7. The children didn't talk in the classroom. They were **quiet** / **quietly**.

B Complete the report card. Use the adverbs of the adjectives in the box.

careful	careless	clear	creative	good
hard	~~neat~~	poor	quick	quiet

To: Ahmed Hassan
Sender: Redwood Middle School
Subject: Report for Tariq Hassan, Fall semester

 Redwood Middle School

Student: Tariq Hassan
Semester: Fall

Subject	Grade	Comments
Language Arts	B	Tariq writes _____neatly_____. His handwriting is always easy to read. He makes a lot of spelling mistakes. He needs to check his spelling_____.
Math	B	Tariq learns _____. He is always the first to solve math problems on the board. Sometimes he works _____. He needs to check his answers for mistakes.
Science	C	Tariq often speaks very _____. It is difficult for other students to hear him. He needs to speak _____ and share his ideas with the class.
Music	D	Tariq does _____ on tests. He got a 65 on his final exam. He needs to study _____ next semester.
Art	A	Tariq thinks _____. He has a great imagination and a lot of new ideas. He follows directions _____. I never have to tell him something twice.

C Complete the conversations. Write the correct object pronouns.

1. **A:** Can you help Lucy with her math problems?

   B: No problem. I'll help ___*her*___.

2. **A:** Mom, I need to go to the library.

   B: OK. I'm busy tonight, but Grandma will take _____.

3. **A:** Alonso, your art project is really good!

   B: Thanks. I worked hard on _____.

4. **A:** I can't remember my spelling words.

   B: All right. Let's review _____ one more time.

5. **A:** Did my teachers talk about _____ at the parent-teacher conference?

   B: Yes, and they had good things to say about you!

D Complete the email. Write the correct object pronouns.

Dear Mom,

　Well, the kids got their report cards from school today. Becky and Mike both did well. I am proud of ___*them*___.
　　　　　　　　　　　　　　　　　　　　　　　　　　　1

　Do you remember last semester? Becky didn't like math. She had trouble with _____.
　　　　　　　　　　　　　　　　　　　　　　　　　　　　　　　　　　　　2
But Becky's teacher, Mr. Molina, was very helpful. Dan and I talked to _____ after
　　　　　　　　　　　　　　　　　　　　　　　　　　　　　　3
school. He told _____ about a new program called Homework Help. Now Becky meets
　　　　　　4
with a student from the high school after class. The student helps _____ with
　　　　　　　　　　　　　　　　　　　　　　　　　　　　　5
homework. This semester, Becky got an A in math! And now she loves _____ !
　　　　　　　　　　　　　　　　　　　　　　　　　　　　　　　6

　Mike also did better this semester. Last semester he got a C in language arts. He
did poorly on his writing assignments. This semester he spent more time on _____.
　　　　　　　　　　　　　　　　　　　　　　　　　　　　　　　　　　　7
He got a B+ ! And Mike made a wonderful science fair project. He really worked hard on
_____. He won second prize!
8
　We are looking forward to your visit next month. We miss _____ !
　　　　　　　　　　　　　　　　　　　　　　　　　9
Love, Karen

A  **DEVELOP YOUR ACADEMIC SKILLS. Read the Academic Skill. Look at the graph in the text.**

The topic of the text will be _____ .

a. problems with attending night courses
b. the benefits of taking daytime classes
c. the different types of courses available

> **Academic Skill: Use information in graphs and tables**
> Authors sometimes use graphs and tables to present information. This information supports the author's main ideas.

B ▶ Listen and read.

COURSE TYPES – PROS AND CONS

For many people, it's hard to work and go to college at the same time. It's also difficult to find time to study if you have children to look after. There are, however, a few different options that may fit your schedule.

5 **NIGHT COURSES**

Night courses are held in the evening. This means people who work during the day can learn after work. Busy parents like these classes, too. It's easier to get childcare in the evening. Evening class sizes are also usually smaller than
10 daytime classes.

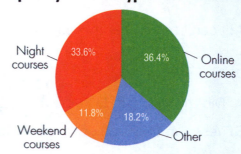

Popularity of course types in the U.S. in 2018

Night courses 33.6%
Online courses 36.4%
Weekend courses 11.8%
Other 18.2%

Note: excluding weekday and daytime courses.

There are problems with night courses, however. If you work all day and then go to class, it can be very tiring. You also have less time to meet friends.

WEEKEND COURSES

If you don't work on the weekend, these can help you avoid very long days of work and study.
15 However, like evening classes, weekend courses also mean you have less time to relax and meet friends and family.

ONLINE COURSES

These are a very popular type of course. You can take online classes anytime of the day, evening, or night. You don't need to travel to and from the school. You also can study anywhere you like — in your own home, in a café,
20 or on a train.

One problem with online courses is that some people like it when a teacher is present. They prefer to talk face-to-face, and to get a quick answer to a question.

C **IDENTIFY. What is the main idea of the article?**

a. Think about your responsibilities and social life before choosing a course type.
b. Avoid night courses if you have to work in the evening.
c. Online courses are good for most types of learners.

D CITE EVIDENCE. Complete the sentences. Where is the information? Write the line number.

Lines

1. Night courses are popular because they _____.
   a. are easier than other classes
   b. fit around work and childcare
   c. are for people who already speak some English   _____

2. Class sizes for night courses are generally _____ those for daytime classes.
   a. smaller than
   b. the same as
   c. bigger than   _____

3. Taking a weekend course may mean you have less time _____.
   a. to study
   b. to work
   c. to spend with friends   _____

4. With an online course, you _____.
   a. have a specific class schedule
   b. can talk face-to-face with a teacher
   c. can study when you like   _____

E INTERPRET. Complete the sentences about the chart.

1. The most popular type of course is _____.
   a. weekday   **b.** night   **c.** online

2. Students prefer not to study _____.
   a. on computers   **b.** on Saturdays and Sundays **c.** in the evening

3. The percentage of students taking online courses is _____ that of students taking night courses.
   a. higher than   **b.** lower than   **c.** the same as

4. 11.8% is the percentage of students who take _____ courses.
   a. night   **b.** weekend   **c.** other

Lessons 8 & 9: Listening and Grammar

A Complete the sentences. Write the possessive forms of the nouns.

1. My (daughter) _daughter's_ teachers are worried about her behavior. She is disrespectful and doesn't pay attention in class.

2. The (children) _____ art projects were all very good. The teacher displayed them in the hallway.

3. Greenville Middle School got money for computers. Now (Ms. Wilson) _____ room has computers for every student.

4. My (son) _____ science grade went from a C to a B. I think he's studying more.

5. The parent-teacher conference was a success. The (parents) _____ attendance was about 90 percent.

6. At the orientation, the principal reviewed the (school) _____ policies about clothes, attendance, and behavior.

7. My (nephew) _____ report card was excellent. He got an A in every subject.

B Add the missing apostrophe to each sentence.

1. Sandra went to her sons' basketball game. The two boys are both on the same team.

2. I'm worried about Marys grades. She got a bad report card this semester.

3. Melissa is a football fan. She knows all the football players names.

4. Jimmy looked at another students paper during the test. His teacher took his paper away and gave him an F.

5. Selim was fooling around in class. The teacher sent him to the principals office.

6. Mr. Murray called Bills parents. He wanted to find out why he wasn't in school.

C Read the article. Cross out the incorrect words.

School Uniforms Debate

Should **students / students'** wear uniforms in school? Students, parents, and teachers have different opinions.

Many parents and teachers like the idea. Parents think uniforms are cheaper than regular **children's / childrens'** clothes. They also think it's easier to get their **kids / kid's** ready for school in the morning. "When I shop for my **kids' / kids** clothes, I don't have to buy expensive designer brands. And my **daughter's / daughters** don't waste so much time in the morning planning what they are going to wear," says Ann Carter, a Greenville mom.

Teachers say that uniforms improve **students' / students** behavior in class. "Wearing a uniform reminds **students /** **students'** that they are in school to learn and that they have to follow the **school's / schools'** rules," says Ted Cezus, a science teacher at Greenville Middle School.

However, most students don't like to wear uniforms. They feel that clothing is a way for people to express their personalities. "I don't want to dress the same as all of my **classmates / classmates'**," explains Tina Lynch, a student at Greenville High School. "I want to wear clothes that show who I am." **Students / Students'** disagree that a **person's / persons'** clothing changes their behavior. "You don't act better because of what you're wearing. You're still the same person inside," says Tina.

D WRITE ABOUT IT. Did you wear a uniform when you were in school? Do you think students should wear uniforms? Explain why or why not.

_____

_____

_____

Lesson 10: Writing

A Read the skill. Check (✓) the correct sentence.

❑ **a.** Her favorite subjects are, art technology and community service.

❑ **b.** Her favorite subjects are art, technology, and community service.

> **Writing Skill: Use commas between words in a list**
>
> Put commas between words in a list. For example:
>
> Most of the school's students come from Mexico, China, and India.

❑ **c.** Her favorite subjects are, art, technology, and community service.

B Read the sentences. Add commas where needed.

1. Ahmad's best subjects are history, science, and English.

2. Mrs. Popov teaches math and music.

3. The children in my son's class speak Spanish Chinese Hindi and Vietnamese.

4. Mr. Rivas said there will be prizes for first second and third in the social studies test.

5. Anna will be busy next week. She has a school play and a science fair.

C Read the text. Correct four more errors.

Greenville Community College is a new school for adults in ~~m~~innesota. It has beginners classes in food preparation, customer service, Chinese language and computer administration. At the end of each course there is a test. Students must study careful to pass. The college principals' name is Mr. Novak. I am take the computer administration course next year so I can find a better job.

Lessons 11: Soft Skills at Work

A **PLANNING AT WORK.** How can you plan well at work? Circle the correct answer.

A person who plans well takes the time to _____.
   a. think ahead and prepare
   b. check over work carefully
   c. come up with creative ideas

Rasha works
in a store.

B Rasha and her manager, Lukas, start their shift. Cross out the incorrect words.
Then circle the correct answer.

1. **Lukas:** I can't believe it's Mother's Day next week! The store **will be / won't be** busy today.

   Rasha: Yes, people will be looking for gifts on their lunch break.

   Lukas: You're right. I think Karima and Emma will need help later.

   Rasha: **I'll / She'll** have my lunch early so I can be here with **them / her**.

   Lukas: Good idea. **That will be / That won't be** really helpful.

2. How does Rasha plan well?

   a. She makes sure there are lots of gifts in the store.

   b. She thinks ahead and solves a problem.

   c. She decides what she will have for lunch.

C Lukas tells Rasha he will be late. Cross out the incorrect words.
Then circle *True* or *False*.

1. **Lukas:** Rasha, I have a **doctor's / doctors'** appointment tomorrow at 10.00. I'll be late to
   work.

   Rasha: Oh, but it's **Nadias / Nadia's** day off. There won't be a manager in the store.

   Lukas: I forgot about that. I'll ask **me / him** for an earlier appointment.

   Rasha: You could do that. Or you could talk to Nadia. Maybe you can change shifts with
   us / her.

   Lukas: Great idea. I didn't think of that.

2. Lukas plans well.   True   False

Unit 10: Let's Eat!

Lesson 1: Vocabulary

A Look at the pictures. Write the food container or quantity. Use the words in the box.

| bag | ~~box~~ | bunch | can | dozen | gallon | half-gallon | jar |

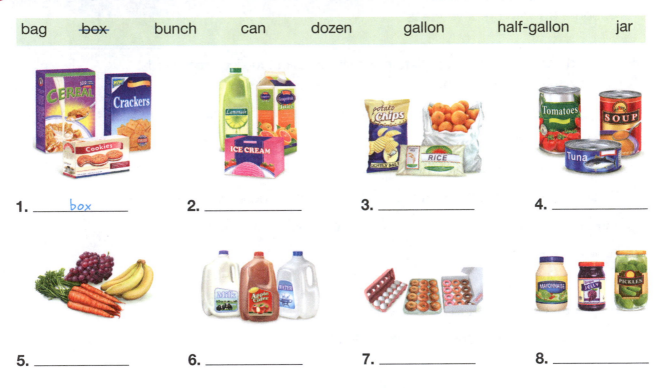

1. _____box_____

2. _____

3. _____

4. _____

5. _____

6. _____

7. _____

8. _____

B Which food matches each container? Circle the correct answer.

1. a bag of _____.

   a. milk   **b.** eggs   **c.** rice

2. a head of _____.

   a. cabbage   **b.** carrots   **c.** ice cream

3. a box of _____.

   a. water   **b.** cookies   **c.** tuna fish

4. a bunch of _____.

   a. grapes   **b.** cereal   **c.** pickles

5. a dozen _____.

   a. donuts   **b.** cheese   **c.** orange juice

6. a gallon of _____.

   a. milk   **b.** tomatoes   **c.** cereal

Lessons 2 & 3: Listening and Grammar

A Complete the chart. Use the words in the box.

~~apple~~	~~fish~~	grape	milk	olive
onion	orange	soda	sugar	yogurt

Count nouns	Non-count nouns
apple	fish

B Write questions with *Is there any/Are there any*. Then look at the picture. Answer the questions with *There's/There are* or *There isn't/There aren't*.

1. **A:** _Is there any_ bread?

   B: _Yes, there's some on the counter._

2. **A:** _____ fish?

   B: _____

3. **A:** _____ apples?

   B: _____

4. **A:** _____ carrots?

   B: _____

5. **A:** _____ yogurt?

   B: _____

6. **A:** _____ bananas?

   B: _____

7. **A:** _____ cheese?

   B: _____

8. **A:** _____ cereal?

   B: _____

C Complete the conversations with *How much* or *How many*.

1. **A:** _____How many_____ carrots do we need?

   B: We don't need any. I bought two bunches of carrots yesterday.

2. **A:** _____ boxes of crackers do we need for the party?

   B: Two boxes are enough.

3. **A:** _____ orange juice should I buy?

   B: None. I think there's a quart in the refrigerator.

4. **A:** _____ lettuce do you need for the salad?

   B: I have one head. I need one more.

5. **A:** _____ jars of jelly did you buy?

   B: I bought three big jars. They were on sale.

D ▶ Listen. Write the words you hear. Then write Paul's shopping list.

Paul: I'm going to the supermarket. Do we need anything for dinner?

Clara: Well. I think I'm going to make some soup. Could you
get some _____?

Paul: Sure. _____ do you need?

Clara: Let me check the recipe. I need _____.

Paul: OK. _____?

Clara: Let's see. _____ carrots?

Paul: Yes, there's _____ carrots in the
refrigerator.

Clara: That's enough. _____ olive oil?

Paul: Yes, there's _____ olive oil in the cabinet.

Clara: Good. _____ potatoes?

Paul: Um. No, there aren't any. I'll get _____.

Shopping List

Lesson 4: Workplace, Life, and Community Skills

A Match the nutrients and the definitions.

1. carbohydrates   _c_   **a.** It is also called *salt*.

2. cholesterol   ___   **b.** It helps your stomach digest food. It comes from plants.

3. fiber   ___   **c.** It gives you energy for several hours.

4. protein   ___   **d.** It gives you quick energy. Too much is not good for you.

5. sodium   ___   **e.** It makes your body strong.

6. sugar   ___   **f.** It is only in animal fat. Too much is not good for you.

B Which food does not belong in each nutrient category? Circle the letter.

1. Fiber

a.

b.

c.

d.

2. Protein

a.

b.

c.

d.

3. Carbohydrates

a.

b.

c.

d.

C Read the labels for two cereal brands on a health blog. Answer the questions.

Toasted Oats

Nutrition Facts

Serving Size 1 Cup (28g)
Servings Per Container 14

Amount Per Serving

Calories 100 Calories from Fat 15

Total Fat 2g

Cholesterol 0mg

Sodium 190mg

Total Carbohydrate 20g

Dietary Fiber 3g

Sugars 1g

Protein 3g

INGREDIENTS: WHOLE GRAIN OATS, CORN STARCH, SUGAR, OAT BRAN, SALT.

Fruit Rings

Nutrition Facts

Serving Size 1 Cup (28g)
Servings Per Container 14

Amount Per Serving

Calories 120 Calories from Fat 10

Total Fat 1g

Cholesterol 0mg

Sodium 135mg

Total Carbohydrate 25g

Dietary Fiber 1g

Sugars 16g

Protein 1g

INGREDIENTS: SUGAR, CORN FLOUR, WHEAT FLOUR, OAT FLOUR, PARTIALLY HYDROGENATED VEGETABLE OIL, SALT, CORN SYRUP, NATURAL AND ARTIFICIAL FLAVOR.

1. What is the main ingredient in Toasted Oats cereal?   *whole grain oats*

2. How much sodium is in one serving of Toasted Oats cereal?   _____

3. How much protein is in one serving of Toasted Oats cereal?   _____

4. How much fiber is in one serving of Toasted Oats cereal?   _____

5. How much sugar is in one serving of Fruit Rings cereal?   _____

6. How many carbohydrates are in one serving of Fruit Rings cereal?   _____

7. How much cholesterol is in one serving of Fruit Rings cereal?   _____

8. How many calories from fat are in one serving of Fruit Rings cereal?   _____

D WRITE ABOUT IT. Search online for the ingredients of your favorite candy bar and a store brand candy bar from a grocery store near you. Write about which ingredients are the same and which are different.

_____

_____

_____

Lessons 5 & 6: Listening and Grammar

A Write the comparative forms of the adjectives. Add *than*.

1. **A:** You're buying frozen pizzas?

   B: Sure. I like them. And they're **(cheap)** ___*cheaper than*___ pizzas from a restaurant.

2. **A:** Want some ice cream?

   B: No, I'm going to have a yogurt. It's **(healthy)** _____ ice cream.

3. **A:** Do you want fresh corn or canned corn?

   B: Fresh corn. Canned vegetables are **(salty)** _____ fresh vegetables.

4. **A:** Should I get beef or fish?

   B: Beef is **(expensive)** _____ and **(fattening)** _____ fish.

   A: OK, let's get fish.

5. **A:** Did you have the chocolate cake or the carrot cake?

   B: I had both. Go for the chocolate. It's **(delicious)** _____ the carrot cake.

B ▶ Listen. Answer the questions. Use a comparative adjective.

Conversation 1

1. Why does Angela like canned soup?

   _____

2. Why does Claudia prefer homemade soup?

   _____

Conversation 2

3. Why does Sam want to eat pizza at The Italian Café?

   _____

4. Why does Ann prefer frozen pizza?

   _____

Conversation 3

5. Why does Sally want to barbecue chicken?

   _____

6. Why does Evan prefer to make sandwiches?

   _____

Lesson 7: Reading

 **A** ▶ Listen and read.

Obesity in the U.S.

Obesity is a big health problem in the U.S. About 40% of adults are very overweight. Almost 19% of children are also obese.

What causes the obesity problem? There are different factors. To begin with, people don't get enough exercise. People are not very active. They no longer walk to the store. Instead they order goods online or they drive to
5 restaurants. Many adults work in offices and sit at desks. Children choose screen time over outdoor activities. They watch movies and play video games. They spend hours online. They don't play outdoor games.

Long working hours is also a factor. Stressed workers are more likely to consume unhealthy products. When people are stressed, they also sleep badly. They then eat too much because they are tired.

The way Americans eat has also changed. People eat out a few times a week. Restaurants serve big portions, so
10 people eat more than they need. When people eat at home, they often eat processed foods. These are quick to prepare. However, they are high in sugar, salt, and fat. Eating too many of these foods causes weight gain.

B **DEVELOP YOUR ACADEMIC SKILLS. Read the Academic Skill. Complete the sentences.**

1. "Obesity is a big health problem in the U.S. About 40% of adults are very overweight."
   Someone who is obese _____.
   a. is healthy
   b. weighs too much
   c. needs to eat more

> **Academic Skill: Get meaning from context**
> You can sometimes guess the meaning of a word from its context (the words and sentences around it).

2. "What causes the obesity problem? There are different factors."
   A factor is _____.
   a. a cause
   b. an ingredient
   c. a result

3. "Restaurants serve big portions, so people eat more than they need."
   A portion is _____.
   a. a serving of food
   b. a meal in a restaurant
   c. unhealthy food

C IDENTIFY. What is the main idea of the article? Circle the correct answer.

   a. Americans eat too much food.
   b. There are many reasons for obesity.
   c. People eat only when they are hungry.

D CITE EVIDENCE. Complete the sentences. Where is the information? Write the line number.

                                                                        Lines
   1. People today don't get enough exercise because _____.
      a. they have become lazier
      b. they spend most of their time at work
      c. they order things online and they drive to restaurants   _____

   2. Children today are less active because _____.
      a. they have too much homework
      b. they eat too much
      c. they watch TV or play video games   _____

   3. People are stressed because _____.
      a. they eat unhealthy foods
      b. they work too much
      c. they are overweight   _____

   4. People often eat too much when they are _____.
      a. at home
      b. stressed and tired
      c. at work   _____

   5. Processed food is _____.
      a. easy to make
      b. high in fiber
      c. healthy   _____

A Cross out the incorrect words.

Server: Are you ready to order?

Ingrid: We need ~~a little~~ / **a few** more minutes.

Server: No problem. Can I answer **any** / **a lot of** questions about the menu?

Ingrid: Do you have **any** / **a little** fish?

Server: We have a fish sandwich. It's here, in the list of lunch specials.

Ingrid: Sounds good. I'd like that.

Server: Would you like **many** / **some** French fries with that?

Ingrid: Could I get **any** / **some** coleslaw instead?

Server: Of course. And for you, sir?

Allen: I'd like the roast chicken.

Server: Would you like **any** / **a lot of** sides with that?

Allen: Mashed potatoes, please.

Server: Anything to drink?

Ingrid: I'll have some iced tea, with just **a little** / **a few** sugar.

Allen: **Any** / **Some** water for me, please.

Server: Sure. I'll be right back with your drinks.

B ▶ Listen. Circle the correct responses.

1. **a.** No, I need a little more time.　　**b.** I'd like some more coffee, please.

2. **a.** Yes. We have apple and orange juice.　　**b.** We have a few apples left.

3. **a.** A hamburger and a side of coleslaw.　　**b.** I'll be right back with your order.

4. **a.** I'd like a soda, please.　　**b.** Some mixed vegetables, please.

5. **a.** A glass of milk, please.　　**b.** I'll have the fish.

C ▶ Listen. Which guest check matches the customers' order? Circle the letter.

Guest Check		
TABLE	SERVER	CHECK #
8	Dan	3268
2	Orange sodas	
1	Macaroni and cheese	
	with onion rings	
1	Roast chicken	
	with coleslaw	
	TAX	
	TOTAL	

a.

Guest Check		
TABLE	SERVER	CHECK #
8	Dan	3268
1	Iced tea	
1	Macaroni and cheese	
	with french fries	
1	Asian noodles	
	with coleslaw	
	TAX	
	TOTAL	

b.

Guest Check		
TABLE	SERVER	CHECK #
8	Dan	3268
2	Orange sodas	
1	Macaroni and cheese	
	with coleslaw	
1	Roast chicken	
	with onion rings	
	TAX	
	TOTAL	

c.

D ▶ Listen. Write the customer's order on the guest check.

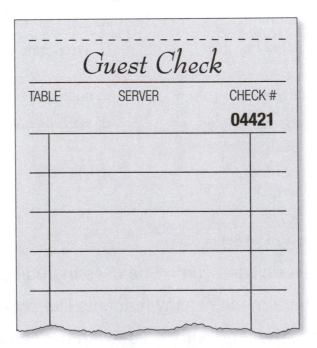

Guest Check		
TABLE	SERVER	CHECK #
		04421

E WRITE ABOUT IT. What is your favorite restaurant? Why do you like it? What foods do you like to order?

_____

_____

_____

Lesson 10: Writing

A Read the writing skill. Circle the words that introduce examples. Underline the examples in each sentence.

> **Writing Skill: Use *like* and *such as* to introduce examples**
>
> Give examples in your writing. Use *like* and *such as* to introduce examples. For example:
>
> Tina cooks meals with healthy ingredients (like) beans and vegetables.
>
> Her food is full of nutrients (such as) protein and fiber.

1. The cake has ingredients (such as) flour, sugar, and eggs.

2. Eggs make a good breakfast. They have healthy nutrients such as protein.

3. Tom eats a healthy lunch. It is low in nutrients like fat and sugar.

4. Pasta with cheese sauce is high in nutrients like carbohydrates and protein.

5. Try not to eat too much fast food like hamburgers and fries.

B Match the sentence halves.

1. Toast with jelly has nutrients   _c_   **a.** such as tea, coffee, and soda.

2. My favorite tomato salad has nutrients   ___   **b.** like potato chips and fries.

3. Caffeine exists in many drinks,   ___   **c.** such as carbohydrates and sugar.

4. The runner eats fish because it is high in nutrients   ___   **d.** such as protein.

5. Children should not eat foods that are high in sodium,   ___   **e.** like fiber.

C Read the text. Correct four more errors.

Sunita likes to cook chicken curry. She uses ingredients like chicken, onions, and yogurt. There are much healthy nutrients like protein, and carbohydrates in the dish. It is healthy than curry made with canned sauce. Sunita's curry does not have unhealthy nutrients such sodium and sugar.

Lesson 11: Soft Skills at Work

A **ASKING FOR HELP AT WORK.** How can you ask for help at work? Check (✓) the correct answers.

❏ **a.** talk to a co-worker about a problem

❏ **b.** do a job even if you don't understand it

❏ **c.** call a supervisor

Anh works in a bakery. She is a sales assistant.

B Anh is serving a customer at work. Cross out the incorrect words. Then circle *True* or *False*.

1. Anh: I'm sorry. Your card isn't working.

Customer: Really? I used it earlier.

Anh: We're having **a few / a little** problems with the machine today. Let me call the credit card company and check for you.

Customer: Thanks.

Anh: Sorry for the delay. Paying by card is usually **more quick / quicker** and **easier / more easier** than using cash.

2. Anh asks for help at work.   True   False

C Anh is serving another customer. Cross out the incorrect words. Then circle *True* or *False*.

1. Customer: Hi, I'd like some donuts for the office, please.

Anh: Sure. How **many / much** boxes would you like?

Customer: Two please. Can I get **many / some** bottles of water, too?

Anh: No problem. So that's a **quart / dozen** donuts and three bottles of water. Is there anything else?

Customer: No, that's it. Hmm, it's **a little / a lot** of stuff to carry. Do you deliver?

Anh: I don't know. I will ask my manager.

2. Anh asks for help at work by looking up information online.   True   False

D **JOB INFORMATION.** Read the information. Then choose *True* or *False*.

Bakers
Bakers make foods like breads and pastries. They work in bakeries, grocery stores, and restaurants. Their shifts are often early mornings, late evenings, weekends, and holidays. They often get training on the job. The training can last a long time.

1. Bakers often work on Saturday.   True   False

2. Bakers need training.   True   False

Lesson 1: Vocabulary

A Look at the pictures. What are the medical emergencies?

She's bleeding.	~~He's choking.~~	She's having trouble breathing.
He's having a heart attack.	She's unconscious.	He's having an allergic reaction.
He swallowed poison.	She burned herself.	He fell.

1. _He's choking._

2. _____

3. _____

4. _____

5. _____

6. _____

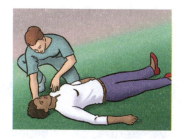  

7. _____

8. _____

9. _____

B Complete the sentences.

1. He's having a   _c_   **a.** breathing.

2. She's having trouble   ___   **b.** allergic reaction.

3. He swallowed   ___   ~~c.~~ heart attack.

4. He's having an   ___   **d.** poison.

5. She burned   ___   **e.** herself.

C ▶ Listen. Complete the conversations.

1. **A:** Would you like eggs for breakfast?

   B: No, I can't eat eggs. If I eat them, I have ___*an allergic reaction*___.

2. **A:** My grandfather went to the hospital this morning.

   B: Oh, no. What's the matter?

   A: He had chest pains. He thought he was having a _____.

3. **A:** Be careful with that knife.

   B: Ow!

   A: Uh-oh. Your finger is _____. Here, let me help you.

4. **A:** Is the soup hot?

   B: Yes, very hot. Don't _____. Let it cool.

5. **A:** There was an ambulance at the café.

   B: Really? What happened?

   A: A woman was _____. She had some food stuck in her throat.

D WRITE ABOUT IT. Write about a time you or someone you know had a medical emergency. What happened?

_____

_____

_____

Lessons 2 & 3: Listening and Grammar

A Complete the conversations. Use the present continuous.

1. **A:** Why _____*is*_____ this little boy (**cry**) ____*crying*____?

   B: His elbow (**bleed**) _____.

2. **A:** _____ you (**feel**) _____ OK? You don't look well.

   B: I don't know what's wrong. I (**have**) _____ trouble breathing.

3. **A:** What (**happen**) _____ downtown?

   B: I'm not sure. There are a lot of fire trucks in the street.

4. **A:** _____ the fire trucks (**come**) _____?

   B: Yes, don't worry. I hear them now.

5. **A:** Why _____ he (**take**) _____ his son to the emergency room?

   B: His son ate some peanuts, and he (**have**) _____ an allergic reaction.

B Complete the conversation. Use the verbs in the box. Change the verbs to the present continuous.

call	happen	~~have~~	lie	talk

A: 9-1-1. What's your emergency?

B: It's my neighbor. She _'s having_ trouble breathing.

A: OK. Tell me what _____. Are you with your neighbor now?

B: Yes, she _____ on the floor of my apartment.

A: Is she unconscious?

B: No, she's awake. My daughters _____ to her.

A: What's your location?

B: 180 Fifth Street. I _____ from Apartment 12 on the second floor.

C Unscramble the questions.

1. (the / What's / emergency) _What's the emergency?_

2. (woman / the / Is / bleeding) _____

3. (the / unconscious / woman / Is) _____

4. (the / of / What's / the / emergency / location) _____

5. (the / What / are / streets / cross) _____

6. (calling / Who / 911 / is) _____

7. (is / now / happening / What) _____

D ▶ Listen to the 911 call. Then answer the questions you wrote in Exercise C.

1. _A woman fell and hit her head._ _____

2. _____

3. _____

4. _____

5. _____

6. _____

7. _____

E WRITE ABOUT IT. Have you or someone you know ever called 911? What was the situation? What questions did the 911 operator ask?

_____

_____

_____

_____

Lesson 4: Workplace, Life, and Community Skills

A ▶ Listen. Complete the fire safety tips.

1. Don't put _____matches_____ where children can get them.

2. Don't put too many electrical _____ in an electrical _____.

3. Don't put an electrical cord under a _____.

4. Don't put a _____ on a lamp. It will get hot and start a fire.

5. Never put a heater close to a _____.

6. Make sure the windows in your house are easy to open. Don't put furniture _____ a window.

FIRE SAFETY TIPS

with Fire Chief
Bill Adams

B Complete the sentences.

escape plan	exits	fire escape
fire extinguisher	~~smoke alarm~~	

1. A _____smoke alarm_____ protects you from fire. It makes a loud noise when there is smoke in the air.

2. It is important to know the location of doors, windows, and stairs. These are the _____ of a building.

3. A _____ is a metal container with water or chemicals in it. You use it to stop a small fire.

4. Many buildings with two or more floors have a _____ on the outside of the building. These stairs lead from a window to the ground.

5. An _____ is a map of a building. It shows how to exit in case of a fire.

C Look at the map of the office. Draw an escape plan for the office. Draw arrows to show all of the exits in each room.

YANG COMPANY ESCAPE PLAN

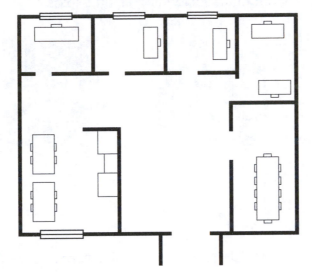

D WRITE ABOUT IT. Draw an escape plan for your workplace or find the map of an office online. Find information about the areas where you need a smoke alarm. How many smoke alarms do you need in total? Where should you put them?

MY WORKPLACE ESCAPE PLAN

MEETING PLACE: _____

Lessons 5 & 6: Listening and Grammar

A Look at the pictures. Write the dangerous situations.

a car accident   a construction accident   an explosion   a robbery

1. _____

   _____

2. _____

   _____

3. _____

   _____

4. _____

   _____

B Look at the news website. Complete the sentences with *there* and *was/wasn't* or *were/weren't*.

REDVILLE HOTEL FIRE   Wednesday, July 2

_____*There was*_____ a fire at the Redville Hotel early this morning. The fire started in the hotel kitchen and moved quickly to the first floor. _____ 245 people inside the hotel at the time of the fire. No one was hurt.

"_____ crowds of people in the street as guests and hotel staff escaped from the hotel," said Fire Chief Ted Cage. "It was lucky that _____ any injuries."

Sunita Thapa works at a convenience store across from the hotel. "I looked up, and I couldn't believe my eyes. _____ fire everywhere. The first floor was burning. _____ people running out of the hotel."

Hotel employee Olga Popov was on the 12th floor when she heard the fire alarm. "_____ a lot of smoke," said Popov. "And the stairs were dark. _____ any light. I'm glad everyone got out OK."

Police closed many streets around the hotel. _____ a traffic jam downtown for several hours after the fire.

A ▶ Listen and read.

FIRST AID – AN IMPORTANT SKILL

You can prevent most emergencies if you follow safety procedures. However, accidents can still happen. In an emergency, you should provide first aid quickly. There are three reasons for this.

1. First aid stops injuries from becoming worse. If someone
5   swallows poison, first aid may reduce the effect.

2. Minutes matter. If you provide first aid quickly, you can keep an injured person stable. For instance, first aid can help a heart attack victim stay alive until an ambulance arrives.

3. Accidents can be stressful. With first aid, you can provide
10   physical comfort. You can offer emotional support, too.

FIRST AID PROCEDURES

Many workplace accidents require first aid. However, you don't need training for all first aid procedures. Here are some simple actions you
15 can take for minor injuries.

Cuts Wash the cut with water. Apply pressure with a bandage. If the blood soaks through, use another bandage. Next, raise the injured body part. This helps to slow down the
20 bleeding. Once the bleeding stops, use a new bandage. If it doesn't stop bleeding, get medical treatment. For deep cuts, first call 911 for help.

Burns First, run cool water over the burn.
25 This will ease the pain. Next, apply a bandage over the burn. This helps to keep it clean. For more severe burns, call 911.

Falls First, ask the person if he or she can move. See if the person is in pain. Look for any injuries or blood. Call 911 if you think the person is badly hurt.

Most serious workplace injuries in the U.S. 2018

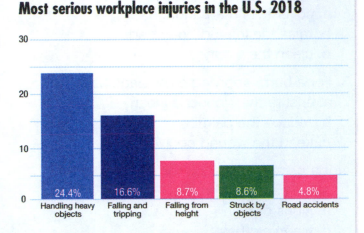

Handling heavy objects	24.4%
Falling and tripping	16.6%
Falling from height	8.7%
Struck by objects	8.6%
Road accidents	4.8%

B DEVELOP YOUR ACADEMIC SKILLS. Read the Academic Skill. Circle the correct answer.

Which of the following sentences supports the idea that "you should provide first aid quickly" in an emergency?

a. "You can prevent most emergencies if you follow safety procedures."

b. "However, accidents can still happen."

c. "First aid stops injuries from becoming worse."

> **Academic Skill: Identify supporting details**
> Authors use supporting details to help explain the main ideas. Supporting details can be reasons, examples, or steps.

C **IDENTIFY.** What is the main idea of the section "First Aid Procedures"? Circle the correct answer.

a. There are basic actions you can take for minor injuries.

b. Always call 911, even for minor injuries.

c. You should complete training before providing any kind of first aid.

D **CITE EVIDENCE.** Complete the sentences. Where is the information? Write the line number.

Lines

1. After an accident, it's important to provide first aid in the
first few _____.
a. seconds
b. minutes
c. hours   _____

2. For a minor cut, you should first _____.
a. cover it with a bandage
b. raise the injured body part
c. clean the wound   _____

3. For a burn, applying a bandage helps to _____.
a. ensure the wound is clean
b. reduce the pain
c. keep the wound cool   _____

4. If a person falls, look for _____.
a. the cause of the fall
b. signs of pain
c. warm clothes   _____

E **INTERPRET.** Complete the sentences about the chart.

1. In 2018, the most common type of workplace injury was caused by _____.
a. handling heavy objects
b. falling and tripping
c. being struck by an object

2. The least likely cause of a workplace injury was by _____.
a. road accidents
b. falling from height
c. falling and tripping

3. The percentage of injuries caused by falling was _____ the percentage of injuries caused
by handling heavy objects.
a. smaller than
b. the same as
c. greater than

Lessons 8 & 9: Listening and Grammar

A ▶ Listen. Complete the conversation.

Officer: Good afternoon. I need to see your _____ and _____.

Driver: OK. Here they are.

Officer: Please _____ and _____. I'll be back in a moment.

[a few minutes later]

Officer: Sir, I pulled you over for _____. I'm giving you a _____ this time. Please drive safely.

B Read the advice about ways to save money on gas. Then combine two imperatives in bold with *and* or *or*.

Dos and Don'ts for Saving Money on Gas

Would you like to save money on gas? If your answer is yes, prepare to change the way you drive. Small changes can save you big money at the gas station. Here are a few tips for the road.

Dos

Drive slower. You will use 23 percent less gas if you drive 55 miles per hour instead of 75 miles per hour.

Stay at the same speed. You use more gas when you change speed often.

Maintain your engine. You use less gas when your engine is working correctly. Follow the maintenance schedule in the owner's manual for your car.

Check the air in your tires. If your tires have too much or too little air, you use more gas. Check them every two weeks.

Turn off the engine. If you have to wait for more than two minutes, turn off the engine and save gas.

Empty your trunk. Heavier cars use more gas than lighter cars. Take everything out of the car that you don't need. Keep your extra tire, though!

Don'ts

Don't start or stop quickly. When you get a green light at traffic light, don't try to speed up too quickly. Sudden stops and starts use more gas.

Don't get stuck in traffic. If you can, avoid driving when there is a lot of traffic. Try to plan trips for when there are fewer cars on the road.

Don't run just one errand. Run many errands at the same time. You can save time and gas!

Don't use the air-conditioning. Use the air-conditioning only when you need it. If it's not that hot, keep it off and save gas.

1. *Drive slower and stay at the same speed.*

2. _____

3. _____

4. _____

5. _____

Lesson 10: Writing

A Read the Writing Skill. Read the text and answer the questions.

My co-worker had an accident last week. She was in the bathroom and slipped on some water. She hit her head and was unconscious for a few minutes. We were very worried. An ambulance came and took her to the hospital. She is better now.

> **Writing Skill: Answer *wh-* questions to give information**
>
> *Wh-* questions begin with words like *who*, *what*, *when*, *where*, *why*, and *how*.
>
> Answer *wh-* questions to give information about an event.
>
> For example: (When) did the accident happen?

1. Who had the emergency?   My co-worker. _____

2. When did it happen?   _____

3. Where did it happen?   _____

4. Why did it happen?   _____

5. What happened?   _____

6. How did she get to the hospital? _____

B Match the questions to the correct answers.

1. Who had the emergency?   __c__   **a.** He is allergic to peanuts.

2. Where did it happen?   ____   **b.** He had an allergic reaction and was taken to the hospital.

3. What happened?   ____   ~~c.~~ My uncle.

4. Why did it happen?   ____   **d.** He is feeling better.

5. How is he now?   ____   **e.** In a restaurant.

C Read the text. Correct four more errors.

Ahmed ~~has~~ *had* an accident last week. He burned his hand where he was in the kitchen. He were watching a video on his laptop. He went to the hospital. There was many people there. He had to sit down or wait for a long time, but his hand is better now.

Lesson 11: Soft Skills at Work

A **SAFETY AT WORK.** How can you follow safety procedures at work? Check (✓) the correct answers.

- ❑ **a.** report accidents to a supervisor
- ❑ **b.** identify fire safety hazards in your workplace
- ❑ **c.** trust that your co-workers will report accidents
- ❑ **d.** wear safety gear if needed

Luis just had an accident at work. He fell off the ladder and hurt his leg.

B Luis talks with Cheng, his supervisor. Cross out the incorrect words. Then circle the correct answer.

1. Luis: Hi, Cheng. Do you have a minute?

Cheng: Yes. Is everything OK?

Luis: No. I just had an **accident / emergency**.

Cheng: Oh no! **What / When** happened?

Luis: I **walked / climbed** to the top of a ladder to get a box and I fell off.

Cheng: Were / Was you hurt?

Luis: I have a small cut on my leg, but it's not **bleeding / bleed** now.

2. Luis followed safety procedures by _____.

a. identifying fire safety hazards

b. reporting accidents to a supervisor

c. wearing safety gear

C Luis talks with Lana, a co-worker. Cross out the incorrect words. Then circle the correct answer.

1. Lana: Hi, Luis. I heard you had an accident. **What / How** did it happen?

Luis: I fell off a ladder and hurt my leg, but it wasn't **serious / injury**. I reported it to the supervisor anyway.

Lana: I had an accident last week, too. I was carrying a box, but it was too **heavy / high** for me. I dropped it and it fell on my foot. It hurt a lot!

Luis: Did you **report / inspect** the accident?

Lana: No. It was my fault. I wasn't wearing my safety **hazard / gear**.

2. What should Lana have done in this situation?

a. Report the accident to her supervisor.

b. Tell other co-workers about the safety hazard.

c. Call 911.

Unit 12: The World of Work

Lesson 1: Vocabulary

A Complete the job responsibilities. Match the words.

1. wear   <u>b</u>   **a.** hands
2. maintain   ___   ~~**b.**~~ gloves
3. wash   ___   **c.** the equipment
4. ask   ___   **d.** late
5. call in   ___   **e.** in/out
6. clock   ___   **f.** questions

B Look at the pictures. Think about each worker's responsibilities. List them below. Use the job responsibilities from Exercise A.

1. _____

2. _____

3. _____

4. _____

5. _____

6. _____

C ▶ Listen to the employees. Match them with their jobs.

1. Nina _____

2. Anthony _____

3. Leona _____

a.

a food service worker

b.

a housekeeper

c.

a construction worker

D Look at the pictures. Think about each worker's responsibilities. List them below.

a server

ask questions

_____

_____

_____

_____

a landscaper

_____

_____

_____

_____

_____

a nurse

_____

_____

_____

_____

_____

Lessons 2 & 3: Listening and Grammar

A Complete the statements. Use *must*, *must not*, *have to*, or *can't* and a verb from the box.

make	park	smoke	wash	~~wear~~

1. All warehouse employees ____*must wear*____ work boots. Warehouse employees _____ sneakers.

2. Employees _____ outside the building in the smoking area. They _____ in the break room.

3. Employees _____ in the employee parking area. Employees _____ in the visitor parking area.

4. Employees _____ personal calls at work. They _____ personal calls at lunch time or during breaks.

5. All employees _____ their hands after using the bathroom.

B ▶ Listen. Complete the sentences with the words you hear.

Greenville Café   Company Policies

1. Employees ____*must park*____ behind the restaurant in the employee parking lot.

2. Employees _____ in or out for other employees.

3. Employees _____ a uniform: a white shirt and black pants.

4. Employees _____ breaks at a scheduled time.

5. Employees _____ a food safety class.

6. Employees _____ to an employee meeting every month.

7. Employees _____ their schedules every Monday.

8. Employees _____ for work more than three times.

Lesson 4: Workplace, Life, and Community Skills

A Look at Trung's pay stub. Match the information on the pay stub with the definitions.

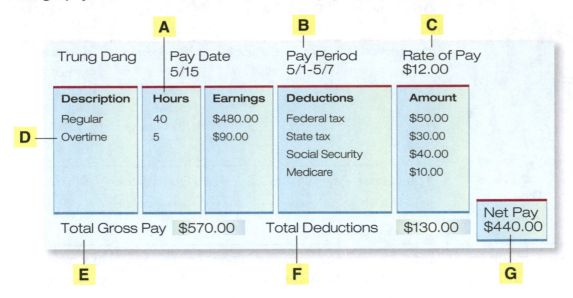

	A		B	C
Trung Dang	Pay Date 5/15		Pay Period 5/1-5/7	Rate of Pay $12.00

Description	Hours	Earnings	Deductions	Amount
Regular	40	$480.00	Federal tax	$50.00
Overtime	5	$90.00	State tax	$30.00
			Social Security	$40.00
			Medicare	$10.00

Total Gross Pay $570.00   Total Deductions $130.00   Net Pay $440.00

D (points to Overtime) **E** (points to Total Gross Pay) **F** (points to Total Deductions) **G** (points to Net Pay)

1. Days Trung worked for this paycheck _____B_____

2. Number of regular hours Trung worked _____

3. Money Trung got before taxes _____

4. Number of overtime hours Trung worked _____

5. Money taken out to pay for taxes and insurance _____

6. Money Trung makes per hour _____

7. Money Trung got after taxes _____

B Look at Trung's pay stub in Exercise A. Complete the sentences.

1. Trung's gross pay is __$570.00__.

2. Trung is paid _____ per hour.

3. Trung worked _____ hours of overtime.

4. Trung's net pay is _____.

5. Trung worked a total of _____ hours.

6. Trung's total deductions are _____.

7. Trung got paid on _____.

8. Trung's federal tax was _____.

C Look at Dina's pay stub. Answer Dina's questions.

Dina

Dina Esteban	Pay Date 11/15		Pay Period 11/1-11/14	Rate of Pay $8.50
Description	**Hours**	**Earnings**	**Deductions**	**Amount**
Regular	40	$340.00	Federal tax	$35.00
Overtime	6	$76.50	Soc. Sec.	$20.00
			Medicare	$10.00
			Health insurance	$30.00

Total Gross Pay $416.50   Total Deductions $95.00   Net Pay $321.50

> How much money did I get paid per hour?

> How much did I get paid for overtime?

> How many overtime hours did I work?

1. _____

2. _____

3. _____

> What is the deduction of $30.00 for?

> When I cash this check, how much money will I get?

> How much federal tax do I pay?

4. _____

5. _____

6. _____

D Read about each worker's schedule and pay. Circle the mistake on each worker's pay stub.

Pablo

> I worked 40 hours. I get paid $14 per hour.

Description	Hours	Rate of Pay	Earnings
Regular	30	$14.00	$490.00

Carlos

> I worked five overtime hours. I get paid $8.00 per hour for that.

Description	Hours	Rate of Pay	Earnings
Regular	40	$7.50	$300.00
Overtime	5	$7.50	$37.50

Lessons 5 & 6: Listening and Grammar

A Write questions with *Who*, *What time*, *Which*, or *Where* and the words in parentheses.

1. **A:** (work) _____ Who worked _____ last weekend?

   B: I think Eric worked on Saturday and Marta worked on Sunday.

2. **A:** (my shift / begin) _____ tomorrow?

   B: At 9:30 A.M. You and Mike are opening the store.

3. **A:** (you / call) _____ about trading shifts?

   B: I called Mike. He said he could work my shift on Friday.

4. **A:** (shift / you / prefer) _____, morning or evening?

   B: I prefer the morning shift. I have to be home with my children at night.

5. **A:** (you / work) _____ on Saturdays?

   B: At a warehouse. I work there part-time on weekends.

6. **A:** (store / close) _____ tonight?

   B: The store closes at 9 P.M., but you need to stay until 10:00 P.M. to help clean up.

B ▶ Listen. Write the question that you hear in each conversation. Then listen again. Answer the questions.

1. **Question:** _Who do I talk to about my schedule?_ _____

   Answer: _Walter, the assistant manager._ _____

2. **Question:** _____

   Answer: _____

3. **Question:** _____

   Answer: _____

4. **Question:** _____

   Answer: _____

C Ask about the underlined information. Write information questions with *Who, What time, When, Which,* or *Where.*

1. **A:** _Which days do you have off?_

   B: I have Friday and Sunday off.

2. **A:** _____

   B: I usually take my break at 3:30.

3. **A:** _____

   B: Daniel traded shifts with me today. I'm going to work for him tomorrow.

4. **A:** _____

   B: Store the safety gear in the cabinet. You can't take it home.

5. **A:** _____

   B: I need time off on Monday and Tuesday. I need to visit my mother in the hospital.

D Read the work schedule. Answer the questions.

	Mon.	Tues.	Wed.	Thu.	Fri.	Sat.	Sun.
Viktor, cashier	OFF	7–3 Break 10–11	7–3 Break 10–11	7–3 Break 10–11	7–3 Break 10–11	7–3 Break 10–11	OFF
Ana, cashier	OFF	OFF	8–4 Break 2–3	8–4 Break 2–3	8–4 Break 2–3	8–4 Break 2–3	8–4 Break 2–3
Frank, grocery department	OFF	10–6 Break 2–3	10–6 Break 2–3	10–6 Break 2–3	OFF	10–6 Break 2–3	10–6 Break 2–3

1. What time does Viktor start work?

   _At 7:00 A.M._

2. When does Ana take a break?

   _____

3. Which days does Frank have off?

   _____

4. What time does Ana get off work?

   _____

5. Who works on Friday?

   _____

6. Who doesn't work on Sunday?

   _____

A DEVELOP YOUR ACADEMIC SKILLS. Read the Academic Skill. Look at the title and pictures in the text. Answer the questions.

Academic Skill: Think about what you know
Before you read, think about what you already know about the topic.

1. The topic of the text is _____.
   a. paycheck deductions
   b. types of income taxes
   c. how to calculate net income

2. Write a sentence about what you already know about this topic.

_____

B ▶ Listen and read.

UNDERSTANDING YOUR PAYCHECK DEDUCTIONS

Do you know where your taxes go? This guide explains the different pay stub deductions.

FEDERAL INCOME TAX
Federal taxes provide money for the U.S. government to run the country.
5 This includes the payrolls of military and federal employees. It is collected by the Internal Revenue Service (IRS). Your rate of federal tax depends on how much you earn. For 2018, it can be between 10 and 37 percent.

STATE INCOME TAX
State taxes are used by a state government. They can also include local county and city taxes. These taxes pay for
10 things such as schools, universities, and state prisons. They also pay for state police and parks. Rates are different from state to state. They are between 0 and 7.5 percent.

FICA
FICA is the Federal Insurance Contributions Act. It requires employers to take Social Security and Medicare tax from your pay. Medicare pays for people aged 65 and over who need medical care. The basic rate is 1.45 percent
15 of your gross pay. You pay 0.9 percent extra if you earn $200,000 or more per year.

SOCIAL DISABILITY INSURANCE (SDI)
This tax provides benefits for disabled workers. Not many states have this tax. It can be between 0.19 and 1.1 percent.

Chen Wong		Pay Date 8/24	Pay Period 8/3–8/10	Rate of Pay $10	
Description	**Hours**	**Earnings**	**Deductions**	**Amount**	
Regular	40	$400.00	Federal tax	$66.00	
Overtime	10	$150.00	State tax	$27.50	
			Social Security	$34.10	
			Medicare	$7.98	
			State Disability Insurance (SDI)	$5.50	**Net Pay**
Total Gross Pay	$550.00		Total Deductions	$141.08	**$408.92**

C IDENTIFY. Complete the sentence.

The main idea of the second paragraph is that federal taxes mainly pay for _____.
  a. military and federal employees
  b. state parks
  c. disability benefits

D CITE EVIDENCE. Complete the sentences. Where is the information? Write the line number.

Lines

1. Federal taxes provides money for _____.
   a. the state government
   b. schools and universities
   c. military and federal employees   _____

2. State income tax _____.
   a. doesn't include city tax
   b. doesn't pay for public schools
   c. pays for parks   _____

3. If you earn $210,000 per year, _____ of your gross pay is
   deducted in Medicare taxes.
   a. 2.35%
   b. 1.45%
   c. 1.1%   _____

4. SDI is mainly used to help people who are _____.
   a. over 65 and need medical care
   b. disabled and can't work
   c. working in the military   _____

E INTERPRET. Complete the sentences about the pay stub in Exercise B.

1. Chen's federal tax rate is _____.
   a. 5%   **b.** 10%   **c.** 12%

2. Chen's state tax rate is _____.
   a. 1%   **b.** 5%   **c.** 6.2%

3. The total tax deductions are _____.
   a. $135.68   **b.** $141.08   **c.** $149.06

4. Chen gets an overtime rate of _____ per hour.
   a. $15   **b.** $16   **c.** $17.50

Lessons 8 & 9: Listening and Grammar

A Complete the conversations. Put the words in order.

1. A: _Could I have next Wednesday night off?_
   (Wednesday / I / night / next / off / could / have)

   B: Of course. No problem.

2. A: _____
   (I / can / to you / for a moment / talk)

   B: Of course. What's up?

3. A: _____
   (I / today / could / a little early / leave work)

   B: OK, but make sure to make up for it tomorrow.

4. A: _____
   (ask you / I / about / some / vacation time / taking / can)

   B: You should talk to Ms. Mills. She usually handles vacation requests.

5. A: _____
   (I / change / to evenings shifts / could)

   B: I'm not sure. I'll look at the schedule next week and see what I can do.

B Rewrite the underlined sentences to ask permission. Change the imperative statements to questions with *Can* or *Could*.

1. I don't know what this word means. <u>Give me your dictionary</u>.

   Could I borrow your dictionary?

2. I have to take my wife to the doctor. <u>Let me have the morning off</u>.

   _____

3. I really want to make some extra money. <u>Give me some overtime hours next week</u>.

   _____

4. Excuse me. <u>I need to ask you something</u>.

   _____

5. It isn't time for my break, but I want to get something to eat. <u>Let me take a break early</u>.

   _____

A Read the Writing Skill. Then read the text and underline the sentences that provide supporting details.

Manufacturing workers have lots of responsibilities. For example, they must always arrive and leave on time. This means they have to clock in and out at the correct time every day. They must also follow health and safety rules. That is, they have to wear safety gear. Finally, they have to treat equipment correctly. This means they must maintain the equipment and report any problems with it.

> **Writing Skill: Give details to support an idea**
>
> Give details to support each idea. Introduce the details with *this means* or *that is*. For example: Nurses have to follow health and safety rules. This means they must wash their hands regularly.

B Match the questions to the correct answers.

> ~~wear safety boots~~   call in late   wear latex gloves
>
> wear an ID badge   ask the right questions

1. Warehouse employees must wear the right clothes. This means they need to _____*wear safety boots*_____.

2. If your car breaks down on your way to work, follow the HR rules. That is, you have to _____.

3. Office workers need to communicate well. This means they must _____.

4. Surgeons have to follow health and safety rules. That is, they must _____.

5. Non-employees are not allowed to enter. This means you always need to _____.

C Read the text. Correct two more errors with how the supporting details are introduced.

Mechanics have several responsibilities. They must follow health and safety rules. ~~Means~~ *This m* they have to report any accidents immediately. They have to use machinery correctly. That's, they need to maintain it regularly. Finally, they need to communicate well. This means, they must follow directions and work as a team.

Lesson 11: Soft Skills at Work

A **BE A TEAM PLAYER AT WORK.** How can you be a team player at work?
Check (✓) the correct answers.

❑ **a.** agree to cover hours for your co-workers

❑ **b.** clarify what a co-worker's responsibilities are

❑ **c.** tell co-workers to ask someone else for help if you're busy

Yuri is a
mechanic.

B Yuri talks with a co-worker. Cross out the incorrect words. Then circle *True* or *False*.

1. Nestor: Yuri, can I speak with you for a minute?

  Yuri: Sure. What's up?

  Nestor: I have to **take / taking** my son to soccer training on Monday. **Could / Would** I

        trade shifts with you?

  Yuri: Oh. I usually have Mondays **on / off**, but OK.

  Nestor: Great! Thanks for covering my **hours / timesheet**.

2. Yuri is a team player.   **True**   **False**

C Yuri talks with another co-worker. Cross out the incorrect words. Then circle *True* or *False*.

1. Yuri: **Can / Will** I ask you a question?

  Rohan: Sorry, my **schedule / shift** is ending soon. I have to go.

  Yuri: It won't take long. I need a week off next month. **How long / Where** do I need

      to be on the job before I can get time off? Six months?

  Rohan: I don't know. Ask someone else.

2. Rohan is a team player.   **True**   **False**

D **JOB INFORMATION.** Read the information. Then choose *True* or *False*.

How to Become an Automotive Mechanic
Most mechanics have a high school degree. Some high schools have classes in automotive repair, electronics, computers, and mathematics. These are useful if you want to become a mechanic. Mechanics also need to complete a program after high school. The program is about automotive service technology. The programs usually are 6 months to a year long. The program has classes and hands-on practice working with cars.

1. Mechanics usually complete a program after high school.   **True**   **False**

2. Math classes in high school can help you become a mechanic.   **True**   **False**

Audio Script

UNIT 1
Page 5, Exercise C

Jack: Hey, Paul. Are you coming to my house for dinner tonight?
Paul: Yeah, thanks for inviting me, Jack.
Jack: I'm inviting Carol, too.
Paul: Carol?
Jack: You know—she has short, curly blond hair.
Paul: Oh. She has blue eyes, right?
Jack: No, she doesn't have blue eyes. She has brown eyes.
Paul: Hmmm. Is she tall?
Jack: Yes, she is. And she's slim.
Paul: Oh, Carol! I know who you're talking about now. She's very pretty.
Jack: Yeah, and she wants to meet you!

UNIT 2
Page 17, Exercise D

A: Where is Roberta?
B: She's at work. She has a new job.
A: Really? Where?
B: She works in a department store.
A: Is it a good job?
B: It's OK. She lives near the store. And the hours are good. She works from 7:30 A.M. to 3:00 P.M.
A: That's good.
B: Yeah. She can take care of her kids when they get home from school.
A: Does her husband still work in a hospital?
B: Yes, he does. He's doing well there.

UNIT 3
Page 31, Exercise C

Irene: I can't wait for Jeff's birthday party tonight! Do I need to bring anything?
Cindy: Well, let's see. Scott is going to get some ice cream on his way home from work. Alex and Nina are going to bring pizza and soda. I'm going to bake a cake.
Irene: Did you remember the decorations?
Cindy: Yes. My sister is going to buy balloons and party games.
Irene: Cake, ice cream, pizza, games . . . sounds like it's going to be a fun party!
Cindy: Oh no! I need to go to the store.
Irene: Why?
Cindy: I forgot something very important. I forgot to buy Jeff 's birthday present!

Page 34, Exercise C

1. A: I need to return these pants.
   B: Why? What's wrong with them?
   A: Look. They're the wrong size.
   B: Wow. They ARE very big!
2. A: Can I help you?
   B: Yes, please. I need to return this jacket.
   A: OK. Is there a problem with the jacket?
   B: Yes, there's a hole in the pocket.
3. A: Are you going to wear your new shirt?
   B: I can't wear it.
   A: Why not?
   B: It's too tight and a seam is ripped.
4. A: I like your new raincoat.
   B: Thanks. I really like it, too. But I need to exchange it.
   A: Why? It fits you well.
   B: I know. But a button is missing.
   A: Oh, too bad.
5. A: What are you doing?
   B: I'm going to the store. I need to return these boots.
   A: How come?
   B: They're too tight. They hurt my feet.

UNIT 4
Page 42, Exercise C

1. A: Greenville Community Center. May I help you?
   B: Uh, hi. Do you have any dance classes?
   A: Dance classes? Yes, we do.
   B: When are they?
   A: Let's see . . . the dance class meets the first and third Monday of the Month from 7:00 to 9:00 P.M.
2. A: Excuse me. My friend needs to learn English. Do you have any classes?
   B: Let me check . . . Yes, we do have an English class.
   A: Great! When is it?
   B: On Tuesday and Thursday evenings.
   A: What time?
   B: It meets from 5:30 to 7:00 P.M.
3. A: Look. There's a new swimming class.
   B: When is it?
   A: Wednesdays at 4 o'clock.
   B: And when does it end?
   A: 6 o'clock.
   B: Great. We should sign the kids up.
4. A: Hey. It says here that there is a Walking Club at the community center. It meets every Sunday. We should go.
   B: Well, I do need some exercise. What time does it meet?
   A: Let's see. . . It meets from 7:00 to 8:00 A.M.
   B: Seven o'clock in the morning . . . on a Sunday!? No way!
5. A: Want to see a movie tomorrow? The community center has a free movie night.
   B: Sounds like fun. When is it?
   A: Every Saturday night at 7:30.

B: Let's go!

Page 44, Exercise C

1. Rick: Hi, Angie.
   Angie: Hi, Rick. Hey, let's do something on Saturday.
   Rick: Sure. Do you want to go hiking? I love hiking.
   Angie: Hiking? I don't know. I don't really like to go hiking. How about going to the beach?
   Rick: To be honest, I hate to go to the beach. There are too many people. And I can't swim!
2. Liz: Let's go out to eat tonight. There's a new Italian restaurant. I heard it's good and not expensive.
   Fred: Sounds great. I love Italian food.
   Liz: Me, too. And we can go dancing after dinner. I love to dance.
   Fred: Me? Go dancing? No thanks.
   Liz: Oh, come on! It'll be fun!
   Fred: No way. I hate to dance

UNIT 5

Page 54, Exercise A

Jackie: Hello?
Charlie: Hi, Jackie. This is Charlie at Richmond Realty. I have a nice apartment to show you.
Jackie: Great! Tell me about it.
Charlie: Well, it's really nice. There are three bedrooms. And there's a large living room.
Jackie: How many bathrooms are there?
Charlie: Two.
Jackie: Is there a dining room?
Charlie: There's no dining room, but there's a big eat-in kitchen.
Jackie: Sounds good. How's the location? Is there a park nearby?
Charlie: Yes, there is. Right around the corner.
Jackie: And is the neighborhood quiet?
Charlie: Yes, it's on a very quiet street. There isn't a lot of traffic.
Jackie: Wow. That sounds perfect. Can I see it today?

Page 59, Exercise B

1. A: I need directions to the library.
   B: OK. At the stop sign, turn left. Then go through two traffic lights.
   A: Thanks.
2. A: Excuse me. Where's the post office?
   B: Go straight. It's on this street.
   A: Thanks very much.
3. A: Where's the pharmacy?
   B: At the traffic light, turn left. It's on the right.
   A: Thank you.
4. A: How do I get to the coffee shop?
   B: Go through two traffic lights. The coffee shop is on the left.

A: Thanks a lot.
5. A: Is there a Chinese restaurant near here?
   B: Yes. Go straight on Pine Street. Go through one traffic light and turn left.
   A: Great!

Page 59, Exercise C

A: Can you give me directions to the hospital?
B: Sure. Go straight on Miller Street.
A: OK. Go straight on Miller Street.
B: Then go through two traffic lights.
A: Go through two traffic lights.
B: Yes. Then turn left onto Ventura Avenue.
A: Turn left onto Ventura Avenue.
B: Exactly. Then go through three stop signs.
A: Go through three stop signs.
B: Yes. The hospital is on the right.
A: Got it. Thanks!

UNIT 6

Page 62, Exercise B

1. A: Mr. Wang, you've worked for this company for 30 years. We're all going to miss you.
   B: Thank you. Thank you very much.
   A: Do you have any plans for the future?
   B: Well, I'm going to go fishing next week.
2. A: Is David coming?
   B: Yes, he's almost here.
   A: He thinks he's coming to see a football game.
   B: There he is! Ssssh!
   All: Surprise!
3. A: Hi, Aunt Martha.
   B: Oh my goodness! Little Johnny! You aren't little anymore!
   A: No, the last time I saw you, I was 10. Now I'm 20.
   B: Look—There are my cousins Joe and Rita! Oh, it's so nice to see everyone again.

Page 63, Exercise B

Rich: How was the family reunion?
Ann: Very nice. We all missed you.
Rich: Yeah. I was sorry I couldn't go. Who was there?
Ann: The whole family showed up. All the aunts, uncles, and cousins.
Rich: Aunt Lucy, too?
Ann: Of course. Everyone listened to her family stories. And we looked at old photos and watched movies of Grandma and Grandpa's wedding.
Rich: Oh yeah? I'm sorry I missed that!
Ann: Well, you should have come! We had a great time. We stayed up late and talked all night.
Rich: Really? I'll definitely have to go next time!

Page 70, Exercise B

Jason had a bad day last Monday. On Sunday night, he stayed up late to watch a movie on TV. He was really tired, so he overslept on Monday morning. Jason got up and got dressed quickly. His wife gave him his lunch, and he ran out the door. But he forgot his wallet. When he got to the bus stop, he didn't have any money for the bus. He ran back to his apartment. He got his wallet and ran out the door again. This time he forgot his lunch. When he got to the bus stop, he jumped on the bus. But he took the wrong bus. He needed to take the number 5 bus, but he took the number 33 bus. He got off the bus and walked to work. When Jason finally got to work, it was 9:45. He was 45 minutes late. At lunch time, Jason was very hungry. He didn't have his lunch, so he went to the candy machine. He put a dollar into the machine, but nothing happened. He lost his money. Jason had to stay late. He had a lot of work to finish. He got home at 7:30. He was hungry and exhausted. He decided that he would stop staying up late on Sunday nights!

UNIT 7

Page 75, Exercise C

Dear Grandma,

We are on vacation this week. Last weekend, we went camping at a state park. We did NOT have a good time. Dad cooked on the campfire every night. The food was really bad. Dad had heartburn, and I had an upset stomach. On Saturday, it rained all day. Mom got sick. She had a sore throat and a cough. On Sunday, Janet and I went swimming. Janet got water in her ear. Now she has an earache. Then Dad and I went hiking. Now I have a rash on my arms and legs. This morning we went to a hotel. No more camping for us!

Love, Marie

Page 78, Exercise D

Pharmacist: Mr. Bronson, your prescription is ready. Is this the first time you are taking Naproxen?

Mr. Bronson: Yes, it is. How much do I take?

Pharmacist: Take two tablets three times a day.

Mr. Bronson: Do I take them with food?

Pharmacist: Yes. Take the tablets at breakfast, lunch, and dinner.

Mr. Bronson: And how long do I take them?

Pharmacist: Ten days.

Mr. Bronson: All right.

Pharmacist: This medicine can make you feel dizzy or nauseous. If this happens, stop taking the medicine and call your doctor.

Mr. Bronson: OK.

Pharmacist: Do you understand these directions?

Mr. Bronson: Yes, I do. Thank you.

UNIT 8

Page 91, Exercise B

Julia came to the U.S. in January, 2016. A month later, she enrolled in an English class. In October, she started nursing classes at the community college. She graduated from nursing school two months ago. Jung-Woo came to the United States in 2014. A year later, he got a job as a server in a restaurant. Two years ago, Jung-Woo got a better job. He is now the assistant manager of a hotel.

Page 94, Exercise B

1. A: Can you work weekends?
   B: Yes, I'm available on Saturdays and Sundays.
   A: We really need someone for both days.
   B: I can do that.
2. A: Can you work first shift or second shift?
   B: When is first shift?
   A: First shift is from 8:00 A.M. to 3:00 P.M.
   B: That's perfect. I need to be home when my kids get out of school at 4 o'clock.
3. A: We need servers for the breakfast shift and the lunch shift. Can you start at 6 A.M.?
   B: No, I can't. I have to take my children to school. But I can work the lunch shift.
4. A: Can you work Monday through Friday?
   B: Yes, I can.
   A: How about weekends?
   B: No, I can't work weekends. I have another job on weekends.
   A: Do you prefer days or evenings?
   B: I prefer days but I can work evenings, too.

UNIT 9

Page 100, Exercise B

Good morning, students. We have a busy week at Greenville Middle School. The Music Club will have a bake sale today. Club members will sell cookies and other baked goods from 11:30 to 12:30 in the cafeteria. The Technology Club will meet in the library today at 4:00. Bad news, Greenville basketball fans. There won't be a basketball game on Wednesday. The Greenville Tigers will play their next home game on Monday at 7:00 P.M. Don't forget there will be a Back-to-school Night for parents on Thursday at 7:30. Your parents will visit your classes and meet your teachers . . . but they won't do your homework for you! And finally, on Friday, the seventh grade class will take a field trip to the Greenville Science Museum. Please remember to bring a bag lunch. Thank you and have a good day.

Page 101, Exercise A

1. Good morning, Redwood Middle School.
2. Oh yes. In Mrs. Miller's class.

3. I'm sorry. She's in class right now. May I take a message?
4. Sure. What's your telephone number?
5. OK, I'll give her the message.

UNIT 10
Page 112, Exercise D
Paul: I'm going to the supermarket. Do we need anything for dinner?
Clara: Well. I think I'm going to make some soup. Could you get some chicken?
Paul: Sure. How much chicken do you need?
Clara: Let me check the recipe. . . . I need a pound of chicken.
Paul: OK. Anything else?
Clara: Let's see. Are there any carrots?
Paul: Yes, there's a bunch of carrots in the refrigerator.
Clara: That's enough. Is there any olive oil?
Paul: Yes, there's a bottle of olive oil in the cabinet.
Clara: Good. Are there any potatoes?
Paul: Um. No, there aren't any. I'll get a pound of potatoes.

Page 115, Exercise B
1. Angela: Hey, Claudia. Let's buy some soup. It's three cans for a dollar.
   Claudia: Actually, Angela, I don't like canned soup. It has too much salt. It's not good for you.
   Angela: Yeah, but it's so convenient. You just open the can and heat it up.
   Claudia: No thanks. I'll make some homemade soup tonight. Forget the cans . . . and the salt.
2. Sam: Let's go out for pizza at The Italian Café.
   Ann: That place is so expensive! I have a pizza in the freezer. I'll make that.
   Sam: Frozen pizza? Come on, Ann! I hate the taste. I want fresh vegetables and cheese.
   Ann: OK, Sam. But you can pay the bill!
3. Sally: Hey, Evan. I've got an idea. Let's barbecue some chicken at your birthday party.
   Evan: I don't know, Sally. That's a lot of work. Let's just make sandwiches. It's easier.
   Sally: Well, that's true, but barbecued chicken is really tasty.

Page 118, Exercise B
1. Are you ready to order?
2. Do you have any fruit juice?
3. What can I get for you?
4. Any sides with that?
5. Can I get you something to drink?

Page 119, Exercise C
Server: Here are your orange sodas. Are you ready to order?
Soo-Jung: Yes, I'll have the macaroni and cheese.
Server: OK. And you get a side with that.
Soo-Jung: Onion rings, please.
Server: And for you, sir?
Chang-Su: I'd like the roast chicken, please.
Server: And what would you like with that?
Chang-Su: A side of coleslaw.
Server: All right. That's one macaroni and cheese with onion rings and one roast chicken with coleslaw.

Page 119, Exercise D
Server: Hi, welcome to Mom's Café. Are you ready to order?
Customer: Yes, I'd like a hamburger.
Server: And what would you like with that?
Customer: French fries, please. And a small salad.
Server: Can I get you anything to drink?
Customer: Do you have bottled water?
Server: Yes, we do.
Customer: Great. I'll have that.
Server: All right. That's a hamburger with a side of French fries, a small salad, and a bottled water.
Customer: That's right.
Server: Very good. I'll be right back with your salad.

UNIT 11
Page 123, Exercise C
1. A: Would you like eggs for breakfast?
   B: No, I can't eat eggs. If I eat them, I have an allergic reaction.
2. A: My grandfather went to the hospital this morning.
   B: Oh, no. What's the matter?
   A: He had chest pains. He thought he was having a heart attack.
3. A: Be careful with that knife.
   B: Ow!
   A: Uh-oh. Your finger is bleeding. Here, let me help you.
4. A: Is the soup hot?
   B: Yes, very hot. Don't burn yourself. Let it cool.
5. A: There was an ambulance at the café.
   B: Really? What happened?
   A: A woman was choking. She had some food stuck in her throat.

Page 125, Exercise D
Operator: 9-1-1. What's your emergency?
Kwan: A woman fell and hit her head. She's bleeding badly.
Operator: Is she unconscious?
Kwan: No, she isn't.
Operator: OK. What's the location of the emergency?

Kwan: I'm in the Golden Apple Restaurant at 1045 North Adams Street.
Operator: What are the cross streets?
Kwan: 25th and 26th Avenues.
Operator: And what's your name?
Kwan: Kwan Park.
Operator: All right, Mr. Park. An ambulance is on its way. But don't hang up. Stay on the line with me until the ambulance gets there.

Page 126, Exercise A

Tina Morales: Is your home safe from fire? This is Tina Green from News 12, and I'm talking to Fire Chief Bill Adams today. Chief Adams, welcome to the program.
Bill Adams: Thank you.
Tina Morales: So, how can we make our homes safe from fire?
Bill Adams: Number one. Be careful with matches. Don't put matches where children can get them.
Tina Morales: Good point.
Bill Adams: And be careful with electrical plugs. Don't put too many electrical plugs in an electrical outlet.
Tina Morales: Electrical plugs can be dangerous.
Bill Adams: Electrical cords can be dangerous, too. Don't put an electrical cord under a rug.
Tina Morales: Any other tips?
Bill Adams: Be careful with lamps. Don't put a cloth on a lamp. It will get hot and start a fire.
Tina Morales: We need to be careful with anything hot.
Bill Adams: That's right. In winter, we have problems with heaters. Never put a heater close to a curtain.
Tina Morales: Keep heaters away from the window curtains.
Bill Adams: And one more safety rule. Make sure the windows in your house are easy to open. Don't put furniture in front of a window. If there's a fire, you want to open the window and get out.
Tina Morales: Important information, Chief. Thanks for talking with us today.

Page 131, Exercise A

Officer: Good afternoon. I need to see your driver's license and registration.
Driver: OK. Here they are.
Officer: Please turn off your engine and stay in your car. I'll be back in a moment.
[a few minutes later]
Officer: Sir, I pulled you over for not wearing a seat belt. I'm giving you a warning this time. Please drive safely

UNIT 12
Page 135, Exercise C

1. Nina: Before I start work, I wash my hands. When I prepare food, I have to wear gloves. And I have to clean the equipment often.
2. Anthony: Hi. I'm Anthony. I build houses. I wear safety gear to protect my head, my eyes, and my hands. I use a lot of tools and equipment. After I finish work for the day, I have to clean my equipment. Then I store the equipment in my truck.
3. Leona: My name is Leona. I work at a hotel. I clock in at 8:00 A.M. and I work until 4:00 P.M. I clean rooms and vacuum the carpets. I have to wear a uniform. After I finish work, I store my equipment in a closet.

Page 136, Exercise B

Welcome to the Greenville Café! Below is a list of our company policies. If you have any questions, please ask your supervisor.
1. Employees must park behind the restaurant in the employee parking lot.
2. Employees must not clock in or out for other employees.
3. Employees have to wear a uniform: a white shirt and black pants.
4. Employees must take breaks at a scheduled time.
5. Employees must pass a food safety class.
6. Employees have to go to an employee meeting every month.
7. Employees have to get their schedules every Monday.
8. Employees can't be late for work more than three times.

Page 139, Exercise B

1. A: I'd like to change my hours next week. Who do I talk to about my schedule?
   B: You should talk to Walter. He's the assistant manager.
   A: OK. Thanks.
2. A: Karen, when do I take my break?
   B: You started today at 9:00. Take your break at 12:30.
   A: All right.
3. A: The new schedule is on the wall.
   B: Oh good. Which days do I have off this week?
   A: Hmm, you have Wednesday and Friday off.
4. A: Excuse me, where is the break room?
   B: It's the second door on the left.
   A: Thanks.

Answer Key

UNIT 1

Page 2, Exercise A

Facial hair	Hair type	Hair length	Height	Weight
a beard	straight	short	average height	average weight
a goatee	curly	long	short	heavy
a mustache	wavy	medium-length	tall	thin

Page 2, Exercise B

Answers will vary.
1. short / straight
2. short / curly
3. long / wavy
4. medium-length / straight

Page 3, Exercise C

Answers will vary.
Michael: short hair, tall, thin, a mustache
Cha-Ram: long hair, straight hair, average weight, short
Alex: curly hair, shoulder-length hair, heavy, average height

Page 4, Exercise A

1. ~~has~~ / have
2. is / ~~has~~
3. are / ~~have~~
4. isn't / ~~aren't~~; ~~don't have~~ / doesn't have
5. doesn't have / ~~don't have~~; is / has

Page 4, Exercise B

1. doesn't have
2. have
3. is
4. has
5. aren't
6. are
7. don't have

Page 5, Exercise C

1. True
2. False
3. False
4. False
5. False
6. True

Page 5, Exercise D

Answers will vary.
1. Marco has short hair.
2. Ernesto has white hair.
3. Lisa is short.
4. Kate has blond hair.
5. Viktor is tall.
6. Olga has short hair.

Page 6, Exercise A

1. apartment
2. date of birth
3. female
4. height
5. weight
6. black
7. brown

Page 6, Exercise B

1. Cruz
2. Clearwater
3. Florida
4. 1978
5. 5 / 6

Page 7, Exercise A

1. and / ~~but~~
2. and / ~~but~~
3. ~~and~~ / but
4. and / ~~but~~
5. ~~and~~ / but
6. and / ~~but~~
7. ~~and~~ / but
8. ~~and~~ / but

Page 7, Exercise B

Answers will vary.
1. Oscar is friendly but he's a little shy. Oscar is funny and he tells great jokes.

2. Chung-Ho is outgoing but she's a little bossy. Chung-Ho is talkative and she likes to tell stories.
3. Jason is shy and he gets nervous when he meets people. Jason loves to travel and visit new places.
4. Meg is hard-working but she likes to relax after work. Meg's husband says she's moody but she's laid-back.

Page 8, Exercise B

1. c   2. b

Page 9, Exercise C

c

Page 9, Exercise D

1. c. Line 4
2. b. Line 14
3. c. "Don't" column, third bullet

Page 9, Exercise E

1. a
2. b
3. a

Page 10, Exercise A

1. Is Pam friendly?
2. Are Mr. and Mrs. Garcia from Mexico?
3. Are you married?
4. Where is your school?
5. How old are the students?
6. Who is your teacher?
7. When is your birthday?
8. What is your name?

Page 10, Exercise B

1. aren't
2. is
3. am not
4. aren't
5. isn't
6. am
7. are

Page 11, Exercise C

1. Where _is Ernesto from?_
2. What _is your phone number?_
3. When _is English class?_
4. How old _is your daughter?_
5. Who _is your manager?_
6. Where _are you from?_

Page 11, Exercise D

Answers will vary.
1. What is your country like?
2. What do you do?
3. How old are you?
4. Do you have children?
5. Are you from Ecuador?
6. Are you married?

Page 12, Exercise A

1. _First_, I take the bus to town, and _then_ I walk to the office.
2. _First_, open the box. _Second_, take out the food. _Then_, put it on the shelf.
3. I speak to the manager and, _after that_, I decide what to do.
4. _To begin_, you log in to your account. _Then_, you post the photo.
5. I walked to the store. _Then_, I went to the doctor. _After that_, I went to the drugstore.

Page 12, Exercise B

This is my routine when I apply for a job I'm interested in. _First_, I read about the company online. _Then_, I find out what skills they are looking for. _Next_, I write a cover letter. _After that_, I send an email to the manager.

Page 12, Exercise C

I _am_ a student. I need to get a new ID card. _First_, I _go_ online to get the form. Then, I put the form in the mail. _After that_, I wait for my ID to arrive.

Page 13, Exercise A

a, c

Page 13, Exercise B

1. Meg: Our work party **is** / ~~are~~ on Saturday night. Are you coming, Ben?

   Ben: ~~No~~ / **Yes**, I am. I can't wait!

   Meg: Great! I have so much to do. ~~Then~~ / **First**, I have to check who can come. After that, I need to find out if we have enough food.

   Ben: Maybe I can help you.

   Meg: Thank you! You are so **supportive** / ~~outgoing~~!

2. True

Page 13, Exercise C

1. Meg: Hi. Did you meet Martin, the new supervisor?

   Cheng: Martin? **Is** / ~~Are~~ he short, with black hair?

   Meg: No, he's tall and he ~~have~~ / **has** red hair.

   Cheng: Oh, no, I didn't meet him, but I saw him this morning.

   Meg: He's nice **and** / ~~but~~ very funny. I can introduce you to him, if you want.

   Cheng: No, thanks. He seems outgoing but very **bossy** / ~~cheerful~~.

2. False

UNIT 2

Page 14, Exercise A

Related by birth: aunt, granddaughter, mother, nephew, niece, sister
Related by marriage: brother-in-law, daughter-in-law, husband, mother-in-law, wife, father-in-law

Page 14, Exercise B

1. husband and wife
2. brother-in-law and sister-in-law
3. sisters
4. mother-in-law and son-in-law
5. mother and daughter
6. brothers
7. aunt and niece
8. grandfather and grandson

Page 15, Exercise C

1. parents
2. children / son and daughter
3. sister-in-law
4. father
5. grandfather
6. brother
7. sister
8. nephew

Page 16, Exercise A

1. lives / works / has
2. live / work / have
3. lives / works / has
4. live / have / work

Page 16, Exercise B

1. Alice and Carlos don't live on Franklin Street.
2. Sophia doesn't work in a hospital.
3. I don't have two jobs.
4. Deshi and Bo don't live in Florida.
5. You don't have four sisters.
6. Martin doesn't live downtown.

Page 17, Exercise C

1. live
2. live
3. lives
4. work
5. doesn't work
6. works
7. have
8. don't have
9. don't have
10. live

Page 17, Exercise D

1. True
2. True
3. False
4. False
5. True

Page 18, Exercise B

1. b   2. c   3. a

Page 19, Exercise C

a

Page 19, Exercise D

1. a. Line 1
2. b. Line 6
3. a. Line 11
4. a. Line 14

Page 20, Exercise A

1. d   2. a   3. e
4. b   5. c

Page 20, Exercise B

1. A: **Do** / ~~Does~~ Jason and I live in Miami?
   B: Yes, we **do** / ~~does~~.
2. A: ~~Do~~ / **Does** Yolanda work for a computer company?
   B: No, she ~~don't~~ / **doesn't**.
3. A: **Do** / ~~Does~~ our parents live near a park?
   B: Yes, they **do** / ~~don't~~.
4. A: ~~Do~~ / **Does** Edward work from 8:00 to 5:00?
   B: No, he ~~don't~~ / **doesn't**.

Page 20, Exercise C

1. A: _Does_ your nephew _live_ in the United States?
   B: Yes, _he does_. My nephew lives here in Phoenix.
2. A: _Do_ you have a brother?
   B: No, _I don't_. I have three sisters.
3. A: _Does_ Nelly _mail_ packages to her family in Puerto Rico?
   B: Yes, _she does_. She mails packages to her family every month.
4. A: _Does_ Hamza _live_ with his cousins?
   B: Yes, he _does_. Hamza lives with his cousins in Chicago.
5. A. _Does_ Simon _have_ any brothers?

   B. Yes, he _does_. He has two brothers.
6. A. _Does_ Alison _work_ in a school?
   B. No, _she doesn't_. She works in an office.

Page 21, Exercise A

1. letter
2. large envelope
3. package

Page 21, Exercise B

Answers will vary.

1. You can send a postcard by ~~Retail Ground~~ _First-Class Mail_.
2. It takes ~~2-9 days~~ _1 day_ for a Priority Mail Express letter to arrive.
3. You can send a ~~90~~ _70_-pound package by Priority Mail.
4. You can send a 12-ounce mailing tube by ~~First-Class Mail~~ _Priority Mail Express or Priority Mail_.
5. With ~~Certified Mail~~ _COD_, the person you send the item to pays the cost of mailing.
6. With ~~Delivery Confirmation~~ _Insurance_, you get money back if the package is lost.

Page 22, Exercise C

1. b   2. b   3. c

Page 22, Exercise D

1. Priority Mail Express Mail, Priority Mail, First- Class Mail / Certified Mail
2. Priority Mail Express Mail, Priority Mail / Insurance

Page 23, Exercise A

1. do – e   4. do – b
2. does – f   5. does – a
3. do – d   6. do – c

Page 23, Exercise B

1. Where does Franco live?
2. When does Dina work?
3. How many cousins do you have?
4. How often does Jackie email her family?
5. Where does your daughter live?
6. How do Mr. and Mrs. Shuh keep in touch with their son?
7. How often does Peter go to class?

Page 24, Exercise A

1. I live in Las <u>V</u>egas, <u>N</u>evada.
2. The food came from <u>N</u>ew <u>O</u>rleans, <u>L</u>ouisiana.
3. The music was popular in <u>C</u>hicago, <u>I</u>llinois.

Page 24, Exercise B

1. Philadelphia, Pennsylvania
2. Chicago, Illinois
3. Miami, Florida
4. Dallas, Texas
5. Los Angeles, California

Page 24, Exercise C

I have two <u>daughters</u>. Maria lives in Mexico City<u>,</u> Mexico and Tina lives in Detroit<u>,</u> Michigan. I live in San Francisco, <u>C</u>alifornia but we keep in touch. We text each other every day. We also talk on the phone on weekends.

Page 25, Exercise A

c

Page 25, Exercise B

1. Supervisor: Bo, **do** / ~~does~~ you have any plans this weekend?

   Bo: Yes, I **do** / ~~does~~. It's my daughter's birthday.

   Supervisor: **When** / ~~Where~~ is it? Dita is sick. She can't work on Saturday.

2. True

Page 25, Exercise C

1. Bo: ~~When~~ / **Where** does your daughter go to college?

    Anna: In California. She ~~live~~ / **lives** in San Diego.

    Bo: **Do** / ~~Does~~ you talk to her every day?

    Anna: No, I **don't** / ~~doesn't~~, but I text her often on my break.

    Bo: It's great that you ~~has~~ / **have** a way to keep in touch.

2. True

Page 25, Exercise D

1. False   2. False

UNIT 3

Page 26, Exercise A

1. a jacket
2. boots
3. jeans
4. a scarf
5. a coat
6. a raincoat
7. a sweatshirt
8. gloves

Page 26, Exercise B

Servet: an umbrella, a shirt, a tie, a suit **or** a jacket
Yasmin: a hat, a sweater, sweatpants, sneakers

Page 27, Exercise A

1. ~~buy~~ / to buy
2. ~~save~~ / to save
3. spend / ~~to spend~~
4. ~~return~~ / to return
5. ~~leave~~ / to leave
6. ~~exchange~~ / to exchange

Page 27, Exercise B

1. doesn't want to buy
2. don't need to return
3. don't need to drive
4. don't want to spend
5. don't want to go

Page 28, Exercise A

1. False   2. False   3. False
4. True   5. True   6. False
7. True

Page 28, Exercise B

1. ClothesMart
2. 20%
3. $40.00
4. 09/07/19
5. $42.40
6. $50.00

Page 29, Exercise C

Circle: women's jacket, men's jacket, women's raincoat

Page 29, Exercise D

1. Discount 10% [should be 25%]
2. No mistakes
3. Discount 20% [should be 30%]
4. $25.00 [should be $15.00]

Page 30, Exercise A

Hi Rosa,
I'm happy you_'re going to visit_ us this weekend! Please come on Sunday because our family _is going to be_ busy on Saturday. We_'re going to do_ some spring cleaning. Lucas _is going to do_ the laundry and I_'m going to clean_ the bathroom. Our kids, Joseph and Manny, _are going to clean_ their rooms. In the afternoon, my mother-in-law _is going to take_ the kids to the movies. Lucas and I _are going to paint_ the living room and wash the floors. The house _is going to look_ beautiful when you see it on Sunday! See you soon!
Eva

Page 30, Exercise B

1. Eva isn't going to relax on Saturday. She's going to be busy.
2. Rosa isn't going to visit on Saturday. She's going to visit on Sunday.
3. The children aren't going to clean the bathroom. They're going to clean their rooms.
4. Eva's mother-in-law isn't going to take Lucas to a movie. She's going to take the kids to a movie.
5. Lucas and Eva aren't going to paint the bedroom. They're going to paint the living room.
6. Lucas and Eva aren't going to wash the floors on Sunday. They're going to wash the floors on Saturday.

Page 31, Exercise C

Irene: I can't wait for Jeff 's birthday party tonight! Do I need to bring anything?

Cindy: Well, let's see. Scott _is going to get_ some ice cream on his way home from work. Alex and Nina _are going to bring_ pizza and soda. I_'m going to bake a cake._

Irene: Did you remember the decorations?

Cindy: Yes. My sister _is going to buy_ balloons and party games.

Irene: Cake, ice cream, pizza, games . . . sounds like it_'s going to be_ a fun party!

Cindy: Oh no! I need to go to the store.

Irene: Why?

Cindy: I forgot something very important. I forgot to buy Jeff 's birthday present!

Page 31, Exercise D

1. Monica is going to clean her house.
2. Pablo and Ana are going to hang out with friends.
3. Ying is going to cook lunch for her kids.

4. James and Bernard are going to go home and relax.
5. Max is going to get lunch at a deli.
6. Carlo is going to wash his car.

Page 32, Exercise B
b

Page 33, Exercise C
b

Page 33, Exercise D
1. a. Line 13
2. b. Line 16
3. c. Line 20
4. b. Line 21

Page 33, Exercise E
1. b   2. a   3. c   4. b

Page 34, Exercise A
1. too / ~~very~~
2. ~~too~~ / very
3. too / ~~very~~
4. ~~too~~ / very; too / ~~very~~
5. too / very; too / very

Page 34, Exercise B
1. too   4. too
2. very   5. very
3. very   6. very

Page 34, Exercise C
1. b   4. a
2. a   5. b
3. b

Page 35, Exercise D
1. The hat is too small.
2. The seam is split.
3. The hat is too big.
4. The pants are too long.
5. The shoes are too big.
6. The pants are too big.
7. The shoes are too small.
8. The jacket is missing a button.

Page 36, Exercise A
1. Topic sentence: If you want to save money, go to many different stores.
2. No topic sentence
3. Topic sentence: Beware of certain costs when shopping online.

Page 36, Exercise B
c.

Page 36, Exercise C
In the past, I spent <u>too</u> much money when I went shopping. Now I'm more careful. First, I don't buy something just because I like it. I might want <u>to</u> buy it, but often I don't really need it. Second, I always check if there <u>is</u> going to be a sale soon in the local stores before paying full price for something. Finally, I always check my change if I pay for something with cash. It's <u>very</u> easy for people to make a mistake.

Page 37, Exercise A
c

Page 37, Exercise B
1. Customer: I ~~want~~ / **want** to get a new tablet. My old one is ~~to~~ / **too** slow.
   Rita: Okay. So you're ~~going~~ / **going to** buy a faster tablet. Is that right?
   Customer: Yes. I hate it when videos take a long time to start playing.
   Rita: Let's see if we can find the right tablet for you. This one is **very** / ~~too~~ fast.
2. True

Page 37, Exercise C
1. Co-worker: I'm ~~too~~ / **very** late for a meeting. I ~~need~~ / **need to** go to the head office. Do you know where it is?
   Rita: I'm ~~going~~ / **going to** check for you. I'll be ~~too~~ / **very** quick.
2. True

Page 37, Exercise D
1. True   2. False

UNIT 4
Page 38, Exercise A
1. go fishing
2. go swimming
3. go out to eat
4. go running
5. go dancing
6. go shopping
7. go for a bike ride
8. go for a walk

Page 38, Exercise B
go: dancing, fishing, running
go to the: beach, zoo, park
go for a: bike ride, walk

Page 39, Exercise A
1. always / ~~never~~, never / ~~always~~
2. ever / ~~often~~
3. usually / ~~never~~
4. sometimes / ~~never~~
5. sometimes / ~~hardly ever~~

Page 39, Exercise B
1. We usually go fishing on Sundays.
2. Benita always goes dancing on Saturday nights.
3. Tom is never on time for work.
4. Ben and Janice go hiking often in the summer. OR Ben and Janice often go hiking in the summer.

5. My father hardly ever goes shopping.

Page 40, Exercise C

1. How often do the children go swimming?
2. How often does the family go for a bike ride?
3. How often does Dina work late?
4. How often do Alfredo and Dina go out to eat?
5. How often does the family visit Grandma?

Page 40, Exercise D

Answers will vary.

1. The children go swimming once a month.
2. The family goes for a bike ride once a week.
3. Dina works late once a month.
4. Alfredo and Dina go out to eat once a month.
5. The family visits Grandma twice a month.

Page 41, Exercise A

1. The ESL class meets on <u>Wednesdays and Fridays</u> from <u>9:00</u> A.M. to <u>12:00</u> P.M.
2. The citizenship preparation class meets every <u>Tuesday</u> at <u>6:30</u> P.M.
3. The Job Interview Workshop meets on the first and third <u>Sunday</u> of the month from <u>8:00 to 10:00</u> P.M.
4. The Resume Writing Workshop starts at <u>11:00</u> A.M. and ends at <u>1:00</u> P.M.

Page 41, Exercise B

1. The Job Application Workshop meets on the first Monday of the month from 8:00 to 11:00 A.M.
2. The Movie Club meets on the second and fourth Sunday of the month from 8:00 to 10:00 P.M.

3. The computer class starts at 1:00 P.M.

Page 42, Exercise C

1. b   2. a   3. a   4. a   5. a

Page 42, Exercise D

Age: Adults   **Topic:** ESL
Time: Evening

Page 43, Exercise A

1. like to take
2. doesn't like to clean
3. hates to iron
4. like to go
5. doesn't like to stay home
6. likes to work
7. hates to get up
8. doesn't like to swim

Page 43, Exercise B

1. likes to
2. like to
3. love to
4. don't like to
5. doesn't like to
6. doesn't like to
7. hates to
8. loves to

Page 44, Exercise C

1.

	Rick	Angie
go hiking	✓	
go to the beach		✓

2.

	Fred	Liz
eat Italian food	✓	✓
go dancing		✓

Page 44, Exercise D

Answers will vary.

1. Matt loves to go fishing.
2. Matt hates to get up early.
3. Matt loves to do karate.
4. Matt hates to go shopping.
5. Matt loves to walk his dog.
6. Matt hates to do citizenship preparation.

Page 45, Exercise A

a

Page 45, Exercise C

a

Page 46, Exercise D

1. c. Line 1
2. c. Line 11
3. b. Line 13
4. a. Line 18

Page 46, Exercise E

1. b   2. a   3. a   4. b

Page 47, Exercise A

1. to cook
2. to meet
3. to exercise
4. to take
5. to pay
6. to get up

Page 47, Exercise B

Chuck: Guess what? I got free tickets to the zoo. Do you and the kids want to go this Saturday?

Melinda: That sounds like fun, but I <u>have to work</u> this Saturday

Chuck: Oh. Do you have any plans on Sunday?

Melinda: Well, I don't, but Barry <u>has to go</u> to his guitar class. And Tina <u>has to play</u> in a soccer game. How about next Saturday? I don't <u>have to work</u> that day.

Chuck: Hmm. Actually, I <u>have to take</u> my mother to a wedding. Can you go on Sunday?

Melinda: No, Sunday's not good. I <u>have to help</u> my sister. She's moving to a new apartment.

Chuck: Oh, well. Too bad.

Page 48, Exercise A

1. I enjoy healthy activities. I _walk to work every day_ and I _use the stairs_ instead of _the elevator_.
2. My job is stressful. I often have to work _extra hours_.
3. I am trying to get in shape. I go _to the gym_ _three times a week_.
4. I like hiking. My friends and I go hiking _in the woods_ _on weekends._

Page 48, Exercise B

I love to go hiking. Every Sunday, my friends and I drive to the mountains nearby. We always bring sandwiches with us. Sometimes we go for a bike ride. We usually get home late in the evening.

Page 48, Exercise C

In my free time, I like _to go_ dancing. I _usually_ go on Friday evening with my sister. My brother hardly _ever_ goes. We _go to_ the school and dance with our friends. The dance _always_ finishes at 10:00 P.M.

Page 49, Exercise A

a, c

Page 49, Exercise B

1. Customer: I ~~am often~~ / often shop here. Can I ask you about something
   Asad: I'm going on my lunch break.
   Customer: It's just a quick question. I ~~love~~ / love to cook pasta, but I can't find any fresh pasta here. Do you know if you sell it?
   Asad: I ~~have~~ / have to go. Ask one of my co-workers
2. False

Page 49, Exercise C

1. Asad: Justin, are you busy?
   Justin: Yes, I ~~have~~ / have to clean the floor. I ~~am usually~~ / usually clean it before I leave.
   Asad: I ~~hate~~ / hate to ask you, but there's a problem with my time sheet. Can you help me with it? I ~~hardly ever~~ / am hardly ever late with it.
   Justin: Okay. I can do it now. And then I ~~have~~ / have to get back to cleaning the floor.
2. True

Page 49, Exercise D

1. True   2. False

UNIT 5

Page 50, Exercise A

1. stuck
2. no heat
3. leaking
4. no hot water
5. working

Page 50, Exercise B

1. The door is stuck.
2. There's no heat.
3. The ceiling is leaking.
4. The toilet is clogged.
5. The faucet is leaking.
6. The washing machine isn't working.

Page 51, Exercise A

1. is / ~~are~~
2. ~~are~~ / am
3. ~~is~~ / are
4. is / ~~are~~
5. ~~is~~ / are
6. ~~am~~ / are
7. is / ~~are~~

Page 51, Exercise B

1. is painting
2. is talking
3. isn't calling; is calling
4. I'm emailing
5. is looking
6. isn't fixing
7. She's buying
8. isn't working
9. is using

Page 52, Exercise A

1. furnished
2. bedroom
3. bathroom
4. apartment
5. floor
6. living room
7. dining room
8. eat-in kitchen
9. heat
10. hot water
11. included
12. washer/dryer
13. basement
14. air-conditioning
15. near
16. transportation
17. month
18. security deposit

Page 52, Exercise B

Answers will vary.
1. The apartment has two bedrooms.
2. The apartment is furnished.
3. The apartment has a small eat-in kitchen.
4. Hot water is not included in the rent.
5. There is air-conditioning.
6. The apartment is near shopping.
7. The security deposit is half of one month's rent.
8. The rent is $1,400 a month.
9. There is parking on the street.

Page 53, Exercise C

1. Water
2. Lin Guo

3. July
4. 30 days
5. 35.6 units
6. By 07/15/2019
7. $187.23

Page 54, Exercise A

Jackie: Hello?

Charlie: Hi, Jackie. This is Charlie at Richmond Realty. I have a nice _apartment_ to show you.

Jackie: Great! Tell me about it.

Charlie: Well, it's really nice. There are three _bedrooms_. And there's a large _living room_.

Jackie: How many _bathrooms_ are there?

Charlie: Two.

Jackie: Is there a dining room?

Charlie: There's no dining room, but there's a big _eat-in kitchen_.

Jackie: Sounds good. How's the location? Is there a park nearby?

Charlie: Yes, there is. Right around the corner.

Jackie: And is the neighborhood quiet?

Charlie: Yes, it's on a very quiet street. There isn't a lot of _traffic_.

Jackie: Wow. That sounds perfect. Can I see it today?

Page 54, Exercise B

1. There _are_ no pets allowed in the building.
2. _Is_ there a supermarket nearby?
3. How many bathrooms _are_ there?
4. There _isn't_ a bus stop near here. / There _is_ no bus stop near here.
5. _Are_ there a lot of stores in the neighborhood?
6. There _are_ three bedrooms.

7. _There's no_ school near here. / There _isn't_ a school near here.
8. _Is_ there a dishwasher?

Page 55, Exercise C

Answers will vary.
1. Is there air-conditioning?
2. Is parking included?
3. Are there shops nearby?
4. Is it near a bus stop?
5. How many bedrooms are there?
6. Is there a laundry room?
7. Is there a lot of traffic on the street?
8. Is there a park nearby?

Page 55, Exercise D

Answers will vary.
1. There is no air-conditioning.
2. There is no parking.
3. There are no shops nearby.
4. There are no parks in the area.
5. It's near a bus stop.
6. It has three bedrooms.
7. It has a laundry room in the basement.
8. There is no traffic on the street.

Page 56, Exercise B

1. a   2. c   3. c   4. b

Page 57, Exercise C

1. a. Line 3
2. c. Line 5
3. b. Line 7
4. c. Line 9
5. c. Line 11

Page 58, Exercise A

1. supermarket
2. high school
3. pharmacy
4. hotel
5. park

Page 59, Exercise B

1. c   2. a   3. b   4. b   5. a

Page 59, Exercise C

Directions to the hospital:
Go straight on Miller Street. _Go through_ two traffic lights. Turn _left_ onto Ventura Avenue.
Go through three _stop signs_. The hospital is on the _right_.

Page 60, Exercise A

[3] My brother is trying to fix it, but he is very slow.
[2] It is leaking and I can't use it.
[1] The sink in my apartment is not working.
[5] He is very helpful and can fix things quickly.
[4] I am calling the building manager later today.

Page 60, Exercise B

[indent] The sink in my apartment is not working. It is leaking and I can't use it. My brother is trying to fix it, but he is very slow. I am calling the building manager later today. He is very helpful and can fix things quickly.

Page 60, Exercise C

My Apartment Search

I like my neighborhood. There are lots of nice apartments for rent. They are large and bright. Some are near the park and school. They all have bus stops nearby. Some of them _have_ parking. The problem is that it _costs_ a lot to live in this area. The rent does not include utilities. We can't spend a lot of money on rent because we are _saving_ to buy our own apartment in _W_ashington. We want to own our home. It is a good investment.

Page 61, Exercise A

a, c

Page 61, Exercise B

1. Yusef: Hi, Omar. **I am** / ~~be~~ calling you with a question.
   Omar: Of course. How can I help?
   Yusef: **There's no** / ~~There aren't any~~ floor cleaner left. **Is there** / ~~Are there~~ another bottle?
   Omar: Yes, **go** / ~~goes~~ down to the basement. There's a bottle on the top shelf.
2. True

Page 61, Exercise C

1. Omar: Good morning, Yusef.
   Yusef: Hello Omar. I am ~~finish up~~ / **finishing up** work now. I did the floors first. Then I cleaned the windows.
   Omar: I didn't know they were dirty! Thanks. ~~Are there~~ / **Is there** anything else you need?
   Yusef: No, I **am doing** / ~~is doing~~ fine now. Thanks.
2. False

Page 61, Exercise D

1. True   2. False

UNIT 6

Page 62, Exercise A

1. a wedding
2. a retirement party
3. a graduation
4. an anniversary party
5. a family reunion
6. a surprise party
7. a funeral

Page 62, Exercise B

1. a retirement party
2. a surprise party
3. a family reunion

Page 63, Exercise A

Amy and Tom <u>stayed</u> at home on Saturday. Amy <u>baked</u> cookies and Tom <u>cleaned</u> the kitchen. They both <u>washed</u> the dishes. Tom <u>fixed</u> a leaking faucet, and Amy <u>painted</u> the front door. They <u>worked</u> hard. In the evening, Amy and Tom <u>wanted</u> to relax, so they <u>watched</u> a movie on TV.
On Sunday, Amy <u>visited</u> her friend. She <u>left</u> early in the morning. Tom <u>decided</u> to stay at home. He <u>called</u> his brother and <u>invited</u> him for coffee at his house. He <u>showed up</u> at one o'clock. They <u>listened</u> to some music and <u>talked</u> all afternoon. Tom's brother <u>needed</u> to get up early the next day, so he <u>didn't stay</u> very late.

Page 63, Exercise B

Rich: How was the <u>family reunion</u>?
Ann: Very nice. We all missed you.
Rich: Yeah. I was sorry I couldn't go. Who was there?
Ann: The whole family <u>showed</u> up. All the aunts, uncles, and cousins.
Rich: Aunt Lucy, too?
Ann: Of course. Everyone listened to her <u>family stories</u>. And we looked at old photos and <u>watched movies</u> of Grandma and Grandpa's wedding.
Rich: Oh yeah? I'm sorry I missed that!
Ann: Well, you should have come! We had a great time. We <u>stayed up late</u> and <u>talked all night</u>.
Rich: Really? I'll definitely have to go next time!

Page 64, Exercise C

Answers will vary.
1. In-Ho and Sun-Ah danced at the barbecue.
2. John cooked hamburgers at the barbecue.
3. Hannah and James talked at the barbecue.
4. David played his guitar at the barbecue.
5. Min-Je and Jae-In played soccer at the barbecue.
6. Judy sang at the barbecue.

Page 65, Exercise A

1. Independence Day
2. Memorial Day
3. Martin Luther King Jr. Day
4. New Year's Day
5. Labor Day
6. Columbus Day
7. Presidents' Day
8. Veterans Day
9. Thanksgiving Day
10. Christmas Day

Page 66, Exercise B

Jan. 1: New Year's Day; **Jan. 21:** Martin Luther King Jr. Day; **Feb. 18:** Presidents' Day; **May 27:** Memorial Day; **Jul. 4:** Independence Day; **Sept. 2:** Labor Day; **Oct. 13:** Columbus Day; **Nov. 11:** Veterans Day; **Nov. 28:** Thanksgiving Day; Dec. 25: Christmas Day

Page 67, Exercise A

1. went
2. didn't get
3. came
4. made
5. grew
6. didn't take
7. got married

Page 67, Exercise B

1. A: <u>Did you have a big wedding?</u>
   B: No, <u>I didn't</u>. I had a small wedding.
2. A: <u>Did you graduate last year?</u>
   B: Yes, <u>I did</u>. I graduated last December.
3. A: <u>Did Anas get a job at a bank?</u>
   B: No, <u>he didn't</u>. He got a job at a school.

4. A: <u>Did Lin meet her husband in 2002?</u>
   B: Yes, <u>she did</u>. They met in January, 2002.
5. A: <u>Did Fatima always want to be a teacher?</u>
   B: No, <u>she didn't</u>. She wanted to be a nurse.
6. A: <u>Did you grow up in a small city?</u>
   B: No, <u>I didn't</u>. I grew up in a big city.

Page 68, Exercise B
b

Page 68, Exercise C
a

Page 69, Exercise D
1. c. Line 3
2. b. Line 1
3. b. Line 7
4. b. Line 9

Page 69, Exercise E
1. c   2. b   3. c

Page 70, Exercise A
1. Why did you oversleep?
2. When did you have car trouble?
3. Where did you find your wallet?
4. What did you do last weekend?
5. Why did you take the wrong bus?
6. What time did you leave work last night?

Page 70, Exercise B
1. Jason overslept because he was really tired. **OR** Jason overslept because he stayed up late to watch a movie on TV.
2. Jason forgot his wallet on his way to work.
3. Jason took the number 33 bus.
4. Jason got to work at 9:45.
5. Jason tried to buy his lunch at the candy machine.

Page 71, Exercise C
Answers will vary.
1. The Carlson family got stuck in traffic.
2. The Carlson family took the wrong exit.
3. The Carlson family forgot their picnic lunch food.
4. The Carlson family lost their car keys.
5. The Carlson family car broke down on the side of a highway.

Page 72, Exercise A
b, e

Page 72, Exercise B
1. In 2011, Maria started teaching.
2. In 1934, Chen moved to the city.
3. We visited my family in 2015.
4. In 1984, Alex got his first bike.
5. In 1993, Mona got a new job.

Page 72, Exercise C
Rohan was born in Mumbai in 1972. He <u>grew up</u> in India but moved to the U.S. to study. In 1995, he <u>graduated</u> from medical school. He worked in a hospital in New York until 2003. Now he works as a doctor in a health center in <u>Chicago</u>.

Page 73, Exercise A
a, b, d

Page 73, Exercise B
1. Chunhua: You asked to see me, Dr. Cruz?
   Dr. Cruz: Yes, can you help ~~I~~ / **me** with something, please?
   Chunhua: Of course. I **will be** / ~~won't be~~ free in 10 minutes.
   Dr. Cruz: Oh, I want to get ~~start~~ / **started** right away.

Chunhua: I'm sorry. I need to finish these charts ~~of~~ / **for** Dr. Lin first.
2. b

Page 73, Exercise C
1. Chunhua: Hi, Martin. Can you cover my shift on Tuesday?
   Martin: Tuesday? Well, I ~~do~~ / **don't** have any plans yet.
   Chunhua: Okay. So you can work on ~~this~~ / **that** day for me?
   Martin: I don't know. I might go to the beach. Can I text you on Tuesday morning?
   Chunhua: That's okay. I'll ask someone ~~other~~ / **else**.
2. False

UNIT 7
Page 74, Exercise A
1. a   2. d   3. g   4. e   5. c
6. h   7. f   8. i   9. b

Page 75, Exercise B
1. a / ~~the~~
2. ~~a~~ / the
3. ~~a~~ / an
4. a / ~~the~~
5. ~~the~~ / (no word)
6. a / ~~(no word)~~
7. ~~a~~ / (no word)
8. ~~a~~ / (no word)
9. a / ~~an~~
10. a / ~~the~~

Page 75, Exercise C
Dear Grandma,
We are on vacation this week. Last weekend, we went camping at a state park. We did NOT have a good time. Dad cooked on the campfire every night. The food was really bad. Dad had <u>heartburn</u>

and I had _an upset stomach_. On Saturday, it rained all day. Mom got sick. She had _a sore throat_ and _a cough_. On Sunday, Janet and I went swimming. Janet got water in her ear. Now she has _an earache_. Then Dad and I went hiking. Now I have _a rash_ on my arms and legs. This morning we went to a hotel. No more camping for us! Love, Marie

Page 76, Exercise A

1. on / ~~in~~
2. at / ~~in~~
3. ~~on~~ / at
4. on / ~~in~~
5. ~~at~~ / from
6. to / ~~by~~
7. ~~from~~ / in

Page 76, Exercise B

1. The appointment is on Thursday.
2. The appointment is on November 19.
3. The clinic opens at 7:00 A.M. on Mondays
4. The clinic closes at 6:00 P.M. on Saturdays.
5. The patient's appointment is in 25 minutes.
6. He should arrive at 3:25 P.M.

Page 77, Exercise A

1. patient
2. expiration date
3. over-the-counter (OTC) medicine
4. prescription
5. dosage
6. refill

Page 77, Exercise B

1. False   4. True
2. True   5. True
3. False

Page78, Exercise C

1. Sarah Carlton
2. Eyes
3. Four drops
4. Every 4 to 6 hours
5. No refills
6. 3/25/2021

Page 78, Exercise D

Pharmacist: Mr. Bronson, your prescription is ready. Is this the first time you are taking Naproxen?

Mr. Bronson: Yes, it is. How much do I take?

Pharmacist: _Take_ two tablets _three_ times a day.

Mr. Bronson: Do I take them with _food_?

Pharmacist: Yes. Take the tablets at breakfast, lunch, and dinner.

Mr. Bronson: And how long do I take them?

Pharmacist: _Ten days._

Mr. Bronson: All right.

Pharmacist: This medicine can make you feel _dizzy_ or nauseous. If this happens, stop taking the medicine and call your _doctor_.

Mr. Bronson: OK.

Pharmacist: Do you understand these _directions_?

Mr. Bronson: Yes, I do. Thank you.

Page 79, Exercise A

1. Maria _had_ a bad accident in her house. She _fell_ down the stairs, and she _sprained_ her arm.
2. Andrew _got_ hurt at work. He _broke_ his ankle, and he _went_ to the emergency room.
3. Fang _got_ sick last week. She _had_ the flu. I _took_ her to the doctor.
4. The new cook _had_ an accident yesterday. She _cut_ her hand with a knife, but she _did not go_ to hospital.
5. Lee _had_ a bad fever last week. He _went_ to the doctor, and _got_ some medicine at the pharmacy.

Page 80, Exercise A

a

Page 80, Exercise C

c

Page 81, Exercise D

1. c. Line 5
2. a. Line 12
3. a. Line 17
4. b. Line 18

Page 81, Exercise E

1. b   2. a   3. c   4. c

Page 82, Exercise A

1. ~~for~~ / because
2. for / ~~because~~
3. for / ~~because~~
4. ~~for~~ / because
5. for / ~~because~~
6. ~~for~~ / because

Page 82, Exercise B

1. My daughter didn't go to school today _because_ she didn't feel well. I went to the drugstore _for_ some flu medicine.
2. Eva took her baby to the clinic _because_ she had a fever. The doctor asked her to come back next week _for_ a blood test.
3. I went to the dental clinic _because_ I needed a checkup. I had to wait a long time _because_ they were very busy.
4. I went to the doctor _for_ a flu shot. I wanted to get the shot _because_ I had the flu last year and I missed a lot of work.

5. Camila always misses class. Last week she was absent _because_ she had a sore throat. Today she's absent _because_ she has to work.

Page 83, Exercise C

Answers will vary.
1. He went to the drugstore because he needed eye drops. / He went to the drugstore for a bottle of eye drops.
2. She missed work because she had a dentist's appointment.
3. He called 911 because he had chest pain.
4. She went to the doctor because she needed a flu shot. / She went to the doctor for a flu shot.
5. He called his supervisor because he had a cold.

Page 84, Exercise A

1. _Maha's son has a rash._ She puts cream on his leg three times a day.
2. I take the medicine at 06:30. _I need to have it one hour before breakfast._
3. Mr. Kumar walks to work every morning. _He needs to exercise._
4. _Martin has a bad cold._ He makes a hot drink with lemon and honey.

Page 84, Exercise B

1. Tam has to stay in bed today _because she has a fever_.
2. Nick is going to be late for his doctor's appointment _because he is stuck in traffic_.
3. Carlos can't go swimming for six weeks _because he has a broken leg_.
4. Olga is not going to give a presentation today _because she has a sore throat_.

Page 84, Exercise C

When I _have_ the flu, I don't go to class. I stay home _because_ I don't want to make other people sick. I rest in bed _from_ morning to evening. I also take a pain reliever _for_ the fever. I _am_ usually better by the next day.

Page 85, Exercise A

a, b

Page 85, Exercise B

1. Belvie: Hi, Maria. How are you?
   Maria: Not good. I ~~have~~ / had a sore throat last night.
   Belvie: Oh! Do you feel better now?
   Maria: Yes, I took medicine **for** / ~~because~~ it. I'm just tired. My shift starts ~~on~~ / **in** ten minutes. I need some coffee!
2. True

Page 85, Exercise C

1. Belvie: The radio was a bit loud this morning. Could you turn it down **in** / ~~at~~ the afternoon?
   Ali: Sure. I thought you liked listening to it.
   Belvie: I usually do, but I ~~have~~ / **had** a headache earlier. The music made my head **hurt** / ~~hurting~~ more.
2. True

Page 85, Exercise D

1. False   2. True

UNIT 8

Page 86, Exercise A

1. d   2. e   3. a
4. f   5. b   6. c

Page 86, Exercise B

1. prepare food
2. unload materials
3. install computer systems
4. record patient information
5. stock shelves
6. supervise employees

Page 87, Exercise C

Answers will vary.
1. **Job title:** food service worker; **Job duties:** prepare food, clean kitchen equipment
2. **Job title:** hospital nurse; **Job duties:** record patient information, look after patients
3. **Job title:** warehouse worker; **Job duties:** unload materials, operate a forklift
4. **Job title:** store clerk; **Job duties:** stock shelves, keep store organized

Page 88, Exercise A

1. can type
2. can't operate
3. can't speak
4. can't use
5. can prepare
6. can order
7. can't lift

Page 88, Exercise B

1. Can you lift heavy boxes?
2. Can Ms. Navarro speak English well?
3. Can Diego order more spaghetti for the kitchen?
4. Can you type?
5. Can David work on Sundays?

Page 89, Exercise C

Answers will vary.
Stock clerk: Can you lift heavy boxes? / Can you order supplies? / Can you operate a forklift?
Cashier: Can you use a cash register? / Can you speak Spanish? / Can you assist customers?

Food service worker: Can you prepare food? / Can you work weekends? / Do you have experience?

Page 89, Exercise D

Answers will vary.

I'm going to give Igor the stock clerk job because he can lift boxes, stock shelves, operate a forklift, and order supplies.

I'm going to give Marie the cashier job because she can use a cash register.

I'm going to give Chan the food service worker job because he can order supplies, prepare food, and clean kitchen equipment.

Page 90, Exercise A

1. False
2. True
3. False
4. False
5. True
6. True
7. True
8. False

Page 90, Exercise B

Answers will vary.

The best match for Gilbert Reyes is the Office Assistant position because he can work full-time in an office, get health benefits, and use a computer.

Page 91, Exercise A

1. in
2. later
3. in
4. In
5. In
6. ago

Page 91, Exercise B

Answers will vary.

Julia:

January, 2016 – came to the U.S.

Februray, 2016 – enrolled in an English class

October, 2016 – started nursing classes

Two months ago from today's date – graduated from nursing school

Jung-Woo:

2014 – came to the U.S.

2015 – got a job as a server in a restaurant

Two years ago from today's date – got a better job in a hotel

Page 92, Exercise A

a

Page 92, Exercise C

c

Page 93, Exercise D

1. c. Line 4
2. b. Line 12
3. a. Line 15
4. b. Line 18
5. a. Line 20

Page 94, Exercise A

1. and
2. or
3. and
4. or
5. or

Page 94, Exercise B

1. Saturday, Sunday
2. first shift
3. lunch shift
4. weekdays, days, evenings

Page 95, Exercise C

Answers will vary.

Coffee Stop Cafe	Employee Schedule		April 7 – April 12				
	Mon.	Tue.	Wed.	Thu.	Fri.	Sat.	Sun.
Morning Shift 6:30 – 11:30 a.m.	Paul	Rosa	Paul	Rosa	Paul	Paul	Paul
Afternoon Shift 11:00 a.m. – 4:00 p.m.	Rosa	Fang	Fang	Fang	Rosa	Fang	Fang

Page 96, Exercise A

1. was / ~~am~~
2. ~~owned~~ / own
3. became / ~~become~~
4. ~~was~~ / am
5. joined / ~~join~~

Page 96, Exercise B

I _worked_ in many jobs. In 2016, I _started_ work as a food service worker. I _cleaned_ kitchen equipment most of the day. After two years, I _became_ a manager. I _manage_ a large team. However, I _am_ ready for a change. Today, I _begin_ night classes.

Page 96, Exercise C

In 2015, I _worked_ in an electronic store in California. I stocked shelves, _helped_ customers, and answered their problems. In 2016, I _went_ to San Jose and worked in a car factory. Last _year_, I _moved_ to Florida and started working in a hotel. I can't wait to _start_ another job soon.

Page 97, Exercise A

a, b, d, e

Page 97, Exercise B

1. Interviewer: Why did you leave your first job?

   Rodrigo: I can / ~~can't~~ explain. I was there for three years and I wanted a change.

   Interviewer: A year ~~last~~ / later, you changed jobs again.

   Rodrigo: Yes, that's right.

   Interviewer: Were you bored again ~~and~~ / or was there another reason?

2. True

Page 97, Exercise C

1. Interviewer: Tell me about your **last** / ~~ago~~ job.
   Rodrigo: I worked as a gardener.
   Interviewer: Did you like that job?
   Rodrigo: Yes. I **can** / ~~can't~~ work outside **and** / ~~or~~ I've always liked growing flowers.

2. c

UNIT 9

Page 98, Exercise A

1. P.E. (physical education)
2. community service
3. language arts/English
4. science
5. art
6. technology
7. social studies/history
8. math
9. music

Page 99, Exercise B

1. art
2. social studies/history
3. math
4. science

Page 99, Exercise C

1. music
2. P.E. (physical education)
3. community service
4. language arts/English
5. technology

Page 100, Exercise A

1. A: won't have   B: will watch
2. A: will be   B: will plan
3. A: will be   B: won't be
4. A: will play   B: will try

Page 100, Exercise B

Good morning, students. We have a busy week at Greenville Middle School. The Music Club _will have_ a bake sale today. Club members _will sell_ cookies and other baked goods from 11:30 to 12:30 in the cafeteria. The Technology Club _will meet_ in the library today at 4:00. Bad news, Greenville basketball fans. There _won't be_ a basketball game on Wednesday. The Greenville Tigers _will play_ their next home game on Monday, at 7:00 P.M. Don't forget there _will be_ a Back-to-school Night for parents on Thursday at 7:30. Your parents _will visit_ your classes and meet your teachers . . . but they _won't do_ your homework for you! And finally, on Friday the seventh grade class _will take_ a field trip to the Greenville Science Museum. Please remember to bring a bag lunch. Thank you and have a good day.

Page 101, Exercise A

Time: *Answers will vary*, current time
To: Mrs. Miller
From: Maria Pardo
Phone: 718-555-4567
Message: *Answers will vary.* Evan's mother has a question about his science fair project. Please call back.

Page 101, Exercise B

1. False   4. False
2. True   5. False

Page 102, Exercise A

1. good / ~~well~~
2. ~~careful~~ / carefully
3. hard / ~~hardly~~
4. ~~neat~~ / neatly
5. ~~quick~~ / quickly
6. poor / ~~poorly~~
7. quiet / ~~quietly~~

Page 102, Exercise B

Language Arts: neatly / carefully
Math: quickly / carelessly
Science: quietly / clearly
Music: poorly / hard
Art: creatively / well

Page 103, Exercise C

1. her   4. them
2. you   5. me
3. it

Page 103, Exercise D

1. them   4. us   7. them
2. it   5. her   8. it
3. him   6. it   9. you

Page 104, Exercise A

c

Page 104, Exercise C

a

Page 105, Exercise D

1. b. Line 7
2. a. Line 9
3. c. Line 15
4. c. Line 19

Page 105, Exercise E

1. c   2. b   3. a   4. b

Page 106, Exercise A

1. daughter's
2. children's
3. Ms. Wilson's
4. son's
5. parents'
6. school's
7. nephew's

Page 106, Exercise B

1. sons'
2. Mary's
3. players'
4. student's
5. principal's
6. Bill's

Page 107, Exercise C

students / ~~students'~~
children's / ~~childrens'~~
kids / ~~kid's~~
~~kid's~~ / kids'
~~daughter's~~ / daughters
students'/ ~~student's~~
students / ~~students'~~
school's / ~~schools~~
classmates / ~~classmates'~~
Students / ~~Students'~~
~~person's~~ / person's

Page 108, Exercise A

b

Page 108, Exercise B

1. Ahmad's best subjects are history, science, and English.
2. Mrs. Popov teaches math and music.
3. The children in my son's class speak Spanish, Chinese, Hindi, and Vietnamese.
4. Mr. Rivas said there will be prizes for first, second, and third in the social studies test.
5. Anna will be busy next week. She has a school play and a science fair.

Page 108, Exercise C

Greenville Community College is a new school for adults in Minnesota. It has beginners classes in food preparation, customer service, Chinese, and computer administration. At the end of each course there is a test. Students must study _carefully_ to pass. The college _principal's_ name is Mr. Novak. I _will_ take the computer administration course next year so I can find a better job.

Page 109, Exercise A

a

Page 109, Exercise B

1. Lukas: I can't believe it's Mother's Day next week! The store **will be** / ~~won't be~~ busy today.
   Rasha: Yes, people will be looking for gifts on their lunch break.
   Lukas: You're right. I think Karima and Emma will need help later.
   Rasha: **I'll** / ~~She'll~~ have my lunch early so I can be here with **them** / ~~her~~.
   Lukas: Good idea. **That will be** / ~~That won't be~~ really helpful.

2. b

Page 109, Exercise C

1. Lukas: Rasha, I have **a doctor's** / ~~doctors'~~ appointment tomorrow at 10.00. I'll be late to work.
   Rasha: Oh, but it's ~~Nadias~~ / **Nadia's** day off. There won't be a manager in the store.
   Lukas: I forgot about that. I'll ask ~~me~~ / **him** for an earlier appointment.
   Rasha: You could do that. Or you could talk to Nadia. Maybe you can change shifts with ~~us~~ / **her**.

2. False

UNIT 10

Page 110, Exercise A

1. box
2. half-gallon
3. bag
4. can
5. bunch
6. gallon
7. dozen
8. jar

Page 110, Exercise B

1. c	3. b	5. a
2. a	4. a	6. a

Page 111, Exercise A

Count nouns:	Non-count nouns:
apple	fish
grape	milk
olive	soda
onion	sugar
orange	yogurt

Page 111, Exercise B

1. A: _Is there any_ bread?
   B: _Yes, there's some on the counter._
2. A: _Is there any_ fish?
   B: _Yes, there's some in the refrigerator._
3. A: _Are there any_ apples?
   B: _Yes, there are some in the fruit bowl._
4. A: _Are there any_ carrots?
   B: _No, there aren't any carrots._
5. A: _Is there any_ yogurt?
   B: _Yes, there's some in the refrigerator._
6. A: _Are there any_ bananas?
   B: _No, there aren't any bananas._
7. A: _Is there any_ cheese?
   B: _Yes, there's some cheese in the refrigerator._
8. A: _Is there any_ cereal?
   B: _Yes, there's some in the cabinet._

Page 112, Exercise C

1. How many
2. How many
3. How much
4. How much
5. How many

Page 112, Exercise D

Paul: I'm going to the supermarket. Do we need anything for dinner?

Clara: Well. I think I'm going to make some soup. Could you get some _chicken_?

Paul: Sure. _How much chicken_ do you need?

Clara: Let me check the recipe. I need _a pound of chicken_.

Paul: OK. _Anything else?_

Clara: Let's see. _Are there any_ carrots?

Paul: Yes, there's _a bunch of_ carrots in the refrigerator.

Clara: That's enough. _Is there any olive oil?_

Paul: Yes, there's _a bottle of_ olive oil in the cabinet.

Clara: Good. _Are there any_ potatoes?

Paul: Um. No, there aren't any. I'll get _a pound of potatoes_.

Page 113, Exercise A
1. c   3. b   5. a
2. f   4. e   6. d

Page 113, Exercise B
1. c   2. d   3. a

Page 114, Exercise C
1. whole grain oats
2. 190mg
3. 3g
4. 3g
5. 16g
6. 25g
7. 0mg
8. 10

Page 115, Exercise A
1. cheaper than
2. healthier than
3. saltier than
4. more expensive / more fattening
5. more delicious

Page 115, Exercise B
Answers will vary.
1. Canned soup is easier to make than homemade soup.
2. Canned soup has more salt than homemade soup.
3. Pizza at The Italian Café is fresher than frozen pizza.
4. Frozen pizza is cheaper than pizza at The Italian Café.
5. Barbecued chicken is tastier than sandwiches.
6. Sandwiches are easier to make than barbecued chicken.

Page 116, Exercise B
1. b   2. a   3. a

Page 117, Exercise C
b

Page 117, Exercise D
1. c. Line 4
2. c. Line 5
3. b. Line 7
4. b. Line 8
5. a. Line 10

Page 118, Exercise A
Server: Are you ready to order?

Ingrid: We need a little / **a few** more minutes.

Server: No problem. Can I answer **any** / a lot of questions about the menu?

Ingrid: Do you have **any** / a little fish?

Server: We have a fish sandwich. It's here, in the list of lunch specials.

Ingrid: Sounds good. I'd like that.

Server: Would you like many / **some** French fries with that?

Ingrid: Could I get any / **some** coleslaw instead?

Server: Of course. And for you, sir?

Allen: I'd like the roast chicken.

Server: Would you like **any** / a lot of sides with that?

Allen: Mashed potatoes, please.

Server: Anything to drink?

Ingrid: I'll have some iced tea, with just **a little** / a few sugar.

Allen: Any / **Some** water for me, please.

Server: Sure. I'll be right back with your drinks.

Page 118, Exercise B
1. a   2. a   3. a   4. b   5. a

Page 119, Exercise C
a

Page 119, Exercise D

Page 120, Exercise A
1. The cake has ingredients (such as) flour, sugar, and eggs.
2. Eggs make a good breakfast. They have healthy nutrients (such as) protein.
3. Tom eats a healthy lunch. It is low in nutrients (like) fat and sugar.
4. Pasta with cheese sauce is high in nutrients (like) carbohydrates and protein.
5. Try not to eat too much fast food (like) hamburgers and fries.

Page 120, Exercise B

1. c   2. e   3. a   4. d   5. b

Page 120, Exercise C

Sunita likes to cook chicken curry. She uses ingredients like chicken, onions, and yogurt. There are _many_ healthy nutrients like protein and carbohydrates in the dish. It is _healthier_ than a curry made with canned sauce. Sunita's curry does not have unhealthy nutrients _such as_ sodium and sugar.

Page 121, Exercise A

a, c

Page 121, Exercise B

1. Anh: I'm sorry. Your card isn't working.
   Customer: Really? I used it earlier.
   Anh: We're having **a few** / ~~a little~~ problems with the machine today. Let me call the credit card company and check for you.
   Customer: Thanks.
   Anh: Sorry for the delay. Paying by card is usually ~~more quick~~ / **quicker** and **easier** / ~~more easier~~ than using cash.

2. True

Page 121, Exercise C

1. Customer: Hi, I'd like some donuts for the office, please.
   Anh: Sure. How **many** / ~~much~~ boxes would you like?
   Customer: Two please. Can I get ~~many~~ / **some** bottles of water, too?
   Anh: No problem. So that's a ~~quart~~ / **dozen** donuts and three bottles of water, Is there anything else?
   Customer: No, that's it. Hmm, it's ~~a little~~ / **a lot of** stuff to carry. Do you deliver?
   Anh: I don't know. I will ask my manager.

2. False

Page 121, Exercise D

1. True   2. True

UNIT 11

Page 122, Exercise A

1. He's choking.
2. She burned herself.
3. He swallowed poison.
4. She's bleeding.
5. He fell.
6. She's having trouble breathing.
7. She's unconscious.
8. He's having a heart attack.
9. He's having an allergic reaction.

Page 123, Exercise B

1. c   2. a   3. d   4. b   5. e

Page 123, Exercise C

1. an allergic reaction
2. heart attack
3. bleeding
4. burn yourself
5. choking

Page 124, Exercise A

1. A: Why _is_ this little boy _crying_?
   B: His elbow _is bleeding_.
2. A: _Are_ you _feeling_ OK? You don't look well.
   B: I don't know what's wrong. I _am having_ trouble breathing.
3. A: What _is happening_ downtown?
   B: I'm not sure. There are a lot of fire trucks in the street.
4. A: _Are_ the fire trucks _coming_?
   B: Yes, don't worry. I hear them now.
5. A: Why _is_ he _taking_ his son to the emergency room?
   B: His son ate some peanuts, and he _is having_ an allergic reaction.

Page 124, Exercise B

A: 9-1-1. What's your emergency?
B: It's my neighbor. She'_s having_ trouble breathing.
A: OK. Tell me what'_s happening_. Are you with your neighbor now?
B: Yes, she'_s lying_ on the floor of my apartment.
A: Is she unconscious?
B: No, she'_s awake_. My daughters _are talking_ to her.
A: What's your location?
B: 180 Fifth Street. I'_m calling_ from apartment 12 on the second floor.

Page 125, Exercise C

1. What's the emergency?
2. Is the woman bleeding?
3. Is the woman unconscious?
4. What's the location of the emergency?
5. What are the cross streets?
6. Who is calling 911?
7. What is happening now?

Page 125, Exercise D

1. A woman fell and hit her head.
2. Yes, she's bleeding badly.
3. No, she isn't.
4. The Golden Apple Restaurant at 1045 North Adams Street
5. 25th and 26th Avenues.
6. Kwan Park
7. An ambulance is on its way.

Page 126, Exercise A

1. matches
2. plugs / outlet
3. rug
4. cloth
5. curtain
6. in front of

Page 126, Exercise B

1. smoke alarm
2. exits
3. fire extinguisher
4. fire escape
5. escape plan

Page 127, Exercise C

Page 128, Exercise A

1. a robbery
2. an explosion
3. a car accident
4. a construction accident

Page 128, Exercise B

There was a fire at the Redville Hotel early this morning. The fire started in the hotel kitchen and moved quickly to the first floor. *There were* 245 people inside the hotel at the time of the fire. No one was hurt.

"*There were* crowds of people in the street as guests and hotel staff escaped from the hotel," said Fire Chief Ted Cage. "It was lucky *there weren't* any injuries."

Sunita Thapa works at a convenience store across from the hotel. "I looked up and I couldn't believe my eyes. *There*

was fire everywhere. The first floor was burning. *There were* people running out of the hotel."

Hotel employee Olga Popov was on the twelfth floor when she heard the fire alarm. "*There was* a lot of smoke," said Popov. "And the stairs were dark. *There wasn't* any light. I'm glad everyone got out OK."

Police closed many streets around the hotel. *There was* a traffic jam downtown for several hours after the fire.

Page 129, Exercise B

c

Page 130, Exercise C

a

Page 130, Exercise D

1. b. Line 6
2. c. Line 16
3. a. Line 25
4. b. Line 27

Page 130, Exercise E

1. a   2. a   3. c

Page 131, Exercise A

Officer: Good afternoon. I need to see your *driver's license* and *registration*.

Driver: OK. Here they are.

Officer: Please *turn off your engine* and *stay in your car*. I'll be back in a moment.

[a few minutes later]

Officer: I pulled you over for *not wearing a seat belt*. I'm giving you a *warning* this time. Please drive safely.

Page 131, Exercise B

1. Drive slower and stay at the same speed.

2. Maintain your engine and check the air in your tires.
3. Turn off the engine and empty your trunk.
4. Don't start or stop quickly or get stuck in traffic.
5. Don't run just one errand or use the air-conditioning.

Page 132, Exercise A

1. My co-worker.
2. Last week.
3. In the bathroom.
4. She slipped on some water.
5. She hit her head and was unconscious for a few minutes.
6. An ambulance took her to the hospital.

Page 132, Exercise B

1. c   2. e   3. b   4. a   5. d

Page 132, Exercise C

Ahmed *had* an accident last week. He burned his hand *when* he was in the kitchen. He *was* watching a video on his laptop. He went to the hospital. There *were* many people there. He had to sit down *and* wait a long time, but his hand is better now.

Page 133, Exercise A

a, b, d

Page 133, Exercise B

1. Luis: Hi, Cheng. Do you have a minute?

   Cheng: Yes. Is everything OK?

   Luis: No. I just had an **accident** / ~~emergency~~.

   Cheng: Oh no! **What** / ~~When~~ happened?

   Luis: I ~~walked~~ / **climbed** to the top of a ladder to get a box and I fell off.

   Cheng: **Were** / ~~Was~~ you hurt?

Luis: I have a small cut on my leg, but it's not **bleeding** / ~~bleed~~ now.
2. b

Page 133, Exercise C

1. Lana: Hi, Luis. I heard you had an accident. ~~What~~ / **How** did it happen?
   Luis: I fell off a ladder and hurt my leg, but it wasn't **serious** / ~~injury~~. I reported it to the supervisor anyway.
   Lana: I had an accident last week, too. I was carrying a box, but it was too **heavy** / ~~high~~ for me. I dropped it and it fell on my foot. It hurt a lot!
   Luis: Did you **report** / ~~inspect~~ the accident?
   Lana: No. It was my fault. I wasn't wearing my safety ~~hazard~~ / **gear**.
2. a

UNIT 12

Page 134, Exercise A

1. b   4. f
2. c   5. d
3. a   6. e

Page 134, Exercise B

1. wear gloves
2. maintain the equipment
3. ask questions
4. clock in/out
5. wash hands
6. call in late

Page 135, Exercise C

1. a   2. c   3. b

Page 135, Exercise D

Answers will vary.
a waitress:
ask questions
wash hands
clock in and out

a landscaper:
maintain the equipment
report problems with the equipment
follow directions

a nurse:
wear gloves
work as a team
follow directions

Page 136, Exercise A

1. must wear / must not wear
2. have to smoke / can't smoke
3. must park / must not park
4. can't make / must make
5. must wash

Page 136, Exercise B

1. must park
2. must not clock
3. have to wear
4. must take
5. must pass
6. have to go
7. have to get
8. can't be late

Page 137, Exercise A

1. B   5. F
2. A   6. C
3. E   7. G
4. D

Page 137, Exercise B

1. $570.00   5. 45
2. $12.00   6. $130.00
3. five   7. 5/15
4. $440.00   8. $50.00

Page 138, Exercise C

1. $8.50
2. $76.50 or $12.75 per hour
3. 6
4. Health insurance
5. $321.50
6. $35.00

Page 138, Exercise D

Ibrahim: 30 hours
Carlos: overtime rate of pay $7.50

Page 139, Exercise A

1. Who worked
2. What time does my shift begin
3. Who did you call
4. Which shift do you prefer
5. Where do you work
6. What time does the store close

Page 139, Exercise B

1. **Q:** Who do I talk to about my schedule?
   A: Walter, the assistant manager.
2. **Q:** When do I take my break?
   A: Take your break at 12:30.
3. **Q:** Which days do I have off this week?
   A: Wednesday and Friday.
4. **Q:** Where is the break room?
   A: Second door on the left.

Page 140, Exercise C

1. Which days do you have off?
2. What time do you take your break?
3. Who did you trade shifts with?
4. Where do I store safety gear?
5. When do you need time off?

Page 140, Exercise D

1. At 7 A.M.
2. From 2–3 P.M.
3. Mondays and Fridays
4. At 4 P.M.
5. Viktor and Ana
6. Viktor

Page 141, Exercise A

1. a
2. Answers will vary

Page 142, Exercise C

a

Page 142, Exercise D

1. a. Line 5
2. c. Line 10
3. a. Line 15
4. b. Line 17

Page 142, Exercise E

1. c   2. b   3. b   4. a

Page 143, Exercise A

1. Could I have next Wednesday night off?
2. Can I talk to you for a moment?
3. Could I leave work a little early today?
4. Can I ask you about taking some vacation time?
5. Could I change to evening shifts?

Page 143, Exercise B

1. Can / Could I borrow your dictionary?
2. Can / Could I have the morning off?
3. Can / Could I have some overtime hours next week?
4. Can / Could I ask you something?
5. Can / Could I take a break early?

Page 144, Exercise A

Manufacturing workers have lots of responsibilities. For example, they must always arrive and leave on time. This means _they have to clock in and out at the correct time every day._ They must also follow health and safety rules. That is, _they have to wear safety gear._ Finally, they have to treat equipment correctly. _This means they must maintain the equipment and report any problems with it._

Page 144, Exercise B

1. wear safety boots
2. call in late
3. ask the right questions
4. wear latex gloves
5. wear an ID badge

Page 144, Exercise C

Mechanics have several responsibilities. They must follow health and safety rules. _This means_ they have to report any accidents immediately. They have to use machinery correctly. _That is,_ they need to maintain it regularly. Finally, they need to communicate well. This means they must follow directions and work as a team.

Page 145, Exercise A

a, b

Page 145, Exercise B

1. Nestor: Yuri, can I speak with you for a minute?
   Yuri: Sure. What's up?
   Nestor: I have to **take** / ~~taking~~ my son to soccer training on Monday. **Could** / ~~Would~~ I trade shifts with you?
   Yuri: Oh. I usually have Mondays ~~on~~ / **off**, but OK.
   Nestor: Great! Thanks for covering my **hours** / ~~timesheet~~.
2. True

Page 145, Exercise C

1. Yuri: **Can** / ~~Will~~ I ask you a question?
   Rohan: Sorry, my ~~schedule~~ / **shift** is ending soon. I have to go.
   Yuri: It won't take a minute. I need a week off next month. **How long** / ~~Where~~ do I need to be on the job before I can get time off? Six months?
2. False

Page 145, Exercise D

1. True   2. True

Illustration credits: Dataflow International: pp. 2, 3, 5, 6, 8, 13,15, 24, 26, 28, 29, 32, 35, 40, 41, 43, 44, 45, 52, 53, 58, 64, 66, 68, 71, 75, 76, 77, 78, 80, 84, 89, 90, 91, 95, 99, 101, 102, 103, 104, 107, 110, 111, 112, 116, 119, 126, 127, 128, 129, 133, 136, 137,138, 140, 141; Neil Stewart/NSV Productions: pp. 21, 136; ElectraGraphics: pp. 25, 49, 85, 121, 145; Luis Montiel: pp. 50, 110, 128; Anna Veltfort: pp. 83, 84; André Labrie: pp. 84, 135; Steve Schulman: pp. 122;

Photo Credits: Front cover: JHero Images/Getty Images; Manuel Breva Colmeiro/Moment/Getty Images; Asiseeit/E+/Getty Images; Hero Images/Getty Images. Page 5: Shutterstock; 6: Pictrough/123RF; 7 (1): Wavebreak Media Ltd/123RF; 7 (2): Szefei/Shutterstock; 7 (3): ProStockStudio/Shutterstock; 7 (4): Gino Santa Maria/123RF; 8: Josep Suria/Shutterstock; 11: Shutterstock; 12: Elena Elisseeva/Shutterstock; 14 (Daniel): Rido/123RF; 14 (Sandra): Hannamariah/Shutterstock; 14 (Karl): Wavebreak Media Ltd/123RF; 14 (Monica): Corinne PERON/123RF; 14 (Gloria): Ana Bokan/Shutterstock; 14 (John): Lukas_zb/Shutterstock; 14 (Joseph): Dolgachov/123RF; 14 (Sally): Erik Reis/123RF; 14 (Tommy): Maryna Sokolova/123RF; 17: William Perugini/123RF; 18: Iofoto/Shutterstock; 19: NinaViktoria/Shutterstock; 22 (top): Szefei/123RF; 22 (bottom): Samuel Borges Photography/Shutterstock; 26 (1): Elenovsky/Shutterstock; 26 (2): 26kot/Shutterstock; 26 (3): Andy Crawford/Dorling Kindersley/Getty Images; 26 (4): Mares Lucian/Shutterstock 26 (5): Tarzhanova/Shutterstock; 26 (6): OlgaGi/Shutterstock; 26 (7): Tarzhanova/Shutterstock; 26 (8): Hemera Technologies/PhotoObjects. net/Getty Images; 27: Fiphoto/123RF; 29 (woman's jacket): Tarzhanova/Shutterstock; 26 (men's jacket): Elenovsky/Shutterstock; 26 (women's raincoat): Creatas/Getty Images; 26 (children's sweatshirt): Tarzhanova/

Shutterstock; 38 (1): Melanie DeFazio/Shutterstock; 38 (2): Elena Elisseeva/Shutterstock; 38 (3): Tongro Images/Alamy Stock Photo; 38 (4): Comstock/Stockbyte/Getty Images; 38 (5): Purestock/Getty Images; 38 (6): Jack Hollingsworth/Stockbyte/Getty Images; 38 (7): Cathy Yeulet/123RF; 38 (8): Simone van den Berg/Shutterstock; 42: Ammentorp/123RF; 44: Sirtravelalot/Shutterstock; 51: Andrey_Popov/Shutterstock; 57: Ralf Kleemann/Shutterstock; 66: Tele52/Shutterstock; 68: dpa picture alliance/Alamy Stock Photo; 74 (a): Perch Images/Stockbyte/Getty Images; 74 (b): SteveLuker/iStock/Getty Images; 74 (c): Rene Jansa/Shutterstock; 74 (d): DianaLundin/iStock/Getty Images; 74 (e): Tatiana Gladskikh/123RF; 74 (f): 9nong/123RF; 74 (g): Fuse/Corbis/Getty Images; 74 (h: Custom Medical Stock Photo/Alamy Stock Photo; 74 (i): Pumatokoh/Shutterstock; 76: Tele52/Shutterstock; 82: Danilov1991xxx/Shutterstock; 86 (1): Andersen Ross Photography Inc/DigitalVision/Getty Images; 86 (2): Andersen Ross/Stockbyte/Getty Images; 86 (3): GoGo Images Corporation/Alamy Stock Photo; 86 (4): Creatas/Getty Images; 86 (5): Jacobs Stock Photography Ltd/DigitalVision/Getty Images; 86 (6): Colorblind Images LLC/ DigitalVision/Getty Images; 87 (1): Dmitry Kalinovsky/123RF; 87 (2): Wendy Hope/Stockbyte/Getty Images; 87 (3): Paul Bradbury/Caiaimage/Getty Images; 87 (4): Wavebreak Media Ltd/123RF; 89 (stock clerk): Jacobs Stock Photography Ltd/DigitalVision/Getty Images; 89 (cashier): Lisa Young/123RF; 89 food service worker): Andersen Ross Photography Inc/DigitalVision/Getty Images ; 90 (website banner): Goodshoot/Getty Images; 91: Khunaspix/123RF; 92 (top): Stockfour/Shutterstock; 92 (bottom): Antonio Guillem/Shutterstock; 95 (Rosa): Shutterstock; 95 (Fang): XiXinXing/Shutterstock; 95 (Paul): Sam74100/123RF; 98 (1): SpeedKingz/Shutterstock; 98 (2): Fstop123/E+/Getty Images; 98 (3):

Undrey/Shutterstock; 98 (4): Frederic Cirou/PhotoAlto/Getty Images; 98 (5): AVAVA/Shutterstock; 98 (6): Karelnoppe/Shutterstock; 98 (7): Rawpixel.com/Shutterstock; 98 (8): John D. Buffington/DigitalVision/Getty Images; 98 (9): Wavebreak Media Ltd/123RF; 99 (1): Jingjits Photography/Shutterstock; 99 (2): StockImageFactory.com/Shutterstock; 99 (3): Wavebreakmedia/Shutterstock; 99 (4): ESB Professional/Shutterstock; 101: Tele52/Shutterstock; 107: DGLimages/Shutterstock; 113 (1a): Kyselova Inna/Shutterstock; 113 (1b): Moving Moment/Shutterstock; 113 (1c): Valeria Aksakova/123RF; 113 (1d): AmorSt-Photographer/Shutterstock; 113 (2a): AS Food studio/Shutterstock; 113 (2b): Slawomir Fajer/Shutterstock; 113 (2c): Jacek Chabraszewski/Shutterstock; 113 (2d): Topseller/Shutterstock; 113 (3a): MaraZe/Shutterstock; 113 (3b): Sergey Lapin/Shutterstock; 113 (3c): Pikselstock/Shutterstock; 113 (3d): Peter Cripps/123RF; 114: Dan Kosmayer/Shutterstock; 118: Usoltsev Kirill/Shutterstock; 124: Terry Alexander/Shutterstock; 126: Tyler Olson/Shutterstock; 128: Pablo77/Shutterstock; 129: Rido/Shutterstock; 131: Pixel 4 Images/Shutterstock; 132: Pathdoc/Shutterstock; 134 (1): Janie Airey/ Photodisc/Getty Images; 134 (2): Fuse/Corbis/Getty Images; 134 (3): Jupiterimages/Stockbyte/Getty Images; 134 (4): INSADCO Photography/Alamy Stock Photo 134 (5): Taylor Jorjorian/Alamy Stock Photo; 134 (6): Michael Krasowitz/Photographer's Choice/Getty Images; 135 (server): Wavebreakmedia/Shutterstock; 135 (landscaper): Welcomia/123RF; 135 (nurse): Wendy Hope/Stockbyte/Getty Images; 138 (Dina): Creativa Images/Shutterstock; 138 (Pablo): Dmitry Kalinovsky/Shutterstock; 138 (Carlos): Blueskyimage/123RF; 141: Josh randall/Shutterstock; 144: Sabphoto/Shutterstock.